BROKEN SKY

A collection of archived poetry and prose
from the heart, soul, and mind of:

Clyde R. Hurlston

copyright © 2022 by Clyde Hurlston. All rights reserved.
Printed in the United States Of America. This book may not be
reproduced or reprinted, unless in the context of reviews,
without prior approval from the author unless otherwise stated.

On behalf of the author, thank you for your purchase;
And may The Hermetic Principles guide us all

www.clydehurlston.com
facebook.com/adebtpaidinink
@adebtpaidinink

"BROKEN SKY" ART BY MITCH GREEN

CLYDE HURLSTON

"... Was suicidal, high, smoking so much lye
I saw a dead bird flying through a broken sky
Wish I could flap wings and fly away
To where black kings in Ghana stay
So I could get old, my flesh rot away
But that'll be the day when it's peace...

"When everything around me got cloudy
The chair became a king's throne, my destiny found me.
It was clear why the struggle was so painful.
Metamorphosis, this is what I changed to.
And God, I'm so thankful."

-Nas,
from the song "You're Da Man"
off the album, Stillmatic.

I
THE BROKEN
-WINGED BIRD

"Hold fast to dreams, for if dreams die,
life is a broken-winged bird that cannot fly."
-Langston Hughes

CLYDE HURLSTON

"INJURED INNOCENCE"
ART BY VALISA BERNARDINO

DON'T LOOK BACK

As time flew by,
Mistakes were made
You've come to find,
You've lost the games you played
A bridge was burned,
A lesson is what I learned
Now I'm on my knees,
Praying you don't return
You can go, just don't look back
It'll help me keep, my sanity intact
Close your eyes, and dream that I still love you
Then awaken to, the fact that we are through
Let's make believe
That you don't have to leave
And then I'll pretend
There'll be some nights that I won't grieve
But this is all on you
For what you've put me through
After what you did
What else would you have me do
You can go, just do not look back
It'll help me keep, my sanity intact
Close your eyes, and dream that I still love you
Then awaken to, the fact that we are through
I can't believe, what you've done to me
Though I miss the days, when you'd run to me
But that has changed, you saw to that
And that's fine with me, as long as you don't look back
You can go, just do not look back
It'll help me keep, my sanity intact
Close your eyes, and dream that I still love you
Then awaken to, the fact that we are through
Reality, is such a complex thing
So I'll have to live with these memories, and the pain they bring
There was once a time, when I'd do anything just to get you
Now I'm begging the Lord, to help me forget you

CLYDE HURLSTON

BALLAD FOR THE BROKEN-HEARTED

Tears are falling, my heart is calling
For you to return
I watch you leaving, as I sit here grieving
Watch as the bridge shall burn
I don't wanna make this such an issue
So I'll just pretend, that I won't miss you
Pick up the pieces, I'm moving on
Sing myself to sleep, such a soothing song
In front of the world, I will fall apart
Clutching this ballad, for my broken heart
People told me, that you wouldn't hold me
I set out to prove them wrong
You played me, felt like you spayed me
I'd reach out to you, but I am too far gone
I don't wanna make this such an issue
So I'll just pretend, that I won't miss you
Pick up the pieces, I'm moving on
Sing myself to sleep, such a soothing song
In front of the world, I will fall apart
Clutching this ballad, for my broken heart
I gave into you, you pushed me away
Gave my love to you, so far did you stray
But yesterday is gone, all I have is today
Brighter is what it shall be, somehow or someway
I don't wanna make this such an issue
So I'll just pretend, that I won't miss you
Pick up the pieces, I'm moving on
Sing myself to sleep, such a soothing song
In front of the world, I will fall apart
Clutching this ballad, for my broken heart

COME UNDONE

Did I miss something
Or did our signals get crossed
Because I followed your directions
And still I got lost
Breaking and shaking
Is what I'm doing nowadays
Crying and trying
To figure out how I screwed up so many ways
What happened here,
How did we fall apart so fast
Not close to a year,
And it's obvious we're not gonna last
We can't escape fate,
So there's no use in trying to run
It's best if we just hold on,
'Cause we're starting to come undone
Our love was fragile
Who would've thought, it'd break so easily
Never in one million years
Did I picture, you leaving me
Faking and taking
Everything I had, now used up is how I lay
You're dying, I'm flying
Away from broken memories, to see another day
What happened here,
How did we fall apart so fast
Not close to a year,
And it's obvious we're not gonna last
We can't escape fate,
So there's no use in trying to run
It's best if we just hold on,
'Cause we're starting to come undone
Undone, best describes that state that we're in
And now that we've come to an end,
You don't know where to begin
And I don't care, as long as it's far away from me
Cause you left me with scars,

CLYDE HURLSTON

That you are too blinded to see
What happened here,
How did we fall apart so fast
Don't you shed one tear,
They said that it wasn't gonna last
Even though we can't escape fate,
Away from you, is where I'm trying to run
It's best if we just move on,
'Cause we've already come undone

A SEARCH FOR SERENITY

Eyes opened, visions of lust
Arise from the ashes, another tear hits the dust
Memories consume, your touch abound
A search ongoing, has inner peace been found?
Your presence, like warmth on a winter night
Your kiss, in this dark world, like a shining ray of light
Questions unanswered, responses unspoken
A circle of mistrust, has it finally been broken?
With confidence, such as serenity can provide you
Insecurities flee, as I spend this time inside you
The world can gasp, the world can turn
Watch as we become one, watch as bridges shall burn
The world can object, this world can intervene
But no soul as gifted, can paint as blissful of a scene
These emotions shall bloom, like seeds entombed underground
An eternity spent with you, is proof that serenity has been found.

CLYDE HURLSTON

BROKEN VOICE

Down a corridor so cold and pale
Lies a soul so strong yet frail
He lies motionless as minutes past
A sinking feeling shall forever last
Who knows not its rhyme or cause
But between each breath a shallow pause
A soul so pure can weep in pain
In the grips of this solitude again
Who knows his horrors have no bounds
Attentive ears hear no sounds
No one but God hears the cries
Blind to truths, he lies awake to lies
The lies of a life unfulfilled
Inspire tears to join the spilled
What is life without a warm embrace
To see a smile shine upon his face
They say he loves this darkened state
That's why he'll refuse to clean his slate
To start again, to start a new
To be reborn within the heart of you
But do not weep, for you do not care
How your life would be, if he wasn't there
Would you notice as the day went by
That he didn't offer one last goodbye
Were there things you should've have said
It's much too late, your chance is dead
As I return to this cage of mine
Not in flesh, but inside the mind
Just know what he gave, he gave by choice
Now you're left with a song from the broken voice...

A FORCE AS GREAT AS WANT

For centuries, we have tried.
As a society, to seek what we have been denied.
And why?
It is because there has never been a force
As great... as want.
It is more powerful than gravity.
And more invasive than addiction.
Want is a force that no one can resist.
Not even the gods.
But down here, on this miserable spinning ball... we want.
A litany of products
Mixed with a myriad of possibilities.
So many ways to quell the gluttons inside of us.
Wanting every new and shiny thing.
Or the latest trendy name to brand us like cattle.
We are so very greedy.
This desire for more is slowly and steadily leading us to ruin.
But we don't care.
Most of us foolishly believe in a God,
That has left us drunk with the promise of an afterlife.
Leaving us with the arrogance of knowing,
that no matter how much we fuck up this world...
We can venture on, into another one.
So we want this world to end.
Greedily looking to every prophecy and natural disaster as proof,
that a child supposedly born on December 25th will return,
and give us the ultimate gift of everlasting life.
But until then we wait... and wait...
We are the mundane masters of mediocrity.
No matter our status in this fledgling motion picture of life,
there is always something, in our mind's eye, that is greater to attain.

CLYDE HURLSTON

LIVE LIKE THERE'S NO GOD

Do you have any idea how small you are?
Do you have any idea how meaningless your existence is?
...In the grand scheme of things...
You all are like sheep wandering in the fields.
Waiting for your shepherd to return.
But when the dams give way...
And all of the forces you have tried to suppress,
in your youthful hubris,
Come crashing in around you...
What will you have left?
What good will your last name do you then?
How will your giant, shiny rims help you then?
Will the brand names on your chest and ass make you invincible?
What good will your bank account be when the skies are black?
When the water is unfit to drink...
The air is unfit to breathe...
When the land outside your door looks scorched and baron...
You know, like on those commercials where some old man
points out the starved, colored children... and begs you for your change...
What will you do... when your world looks like theirs?
When your prayers go unanswered?
When your supposed God allows your car... your home...
and your pretty, picket fence... to go the way of Atlantis?
What will you do?
I'll tell you what you'll do...
You'll gather the few that you trust...
The few that you care for...
And you will gather...
You will pray...
You will foolishly find your strength in numbers...
Much like ants on a leaf... as they float away down the flooded streets...
In your hopelessness, you will look skyward...
And with your eyes not in front...
And your eyes not in the back of your head...
You will make yourselves easier to slaughter...

BROKEN SKY

After all...
Isn't that what sheep are made for?
Isn't that why your shepherd was a lamb?
To show you how easy it is... to be at the mercy of the "righteous?'
To show you how beautiful the world is...
when it's reflected on the face of glass houses?
Ha ha ha ha ha ha ha ha ha ha
Come now, my friend...
I'm not throwing stones.
We're merely talking here.
Aren't we?
No, I guess not.
It's just me talking.
But I hope you're listening...
I hope when the world begins to end... your facade will as well...
See... the things you need a reason for... I just do.
You have to smoke something to ease your pain...
You have to drink something to loosen your tongue...
And you might need both to have the courage to fuck someone...
Me? I've long since embraced my pain.
Me? I have to remind myself to hold my tongue.
And me? I only need a willing partner to fuck someone...
But no, we here at the bottom are not supermodels or musclebound...
The things I'm saying now, may make you shudder in disgust
To picture this body of mine doing them...
But that's okay...
I'm free in all the ways you are not...
You're always at the mercy of something...
Your fears... your kids... your fellow churchgoers...
Whether you're in the big city or some small, backwood town...
You are a slave to the opinion of others...
No matter how much you give... now matter how much you volunteer...
They will always whisper behind your back...
No matter if they turn around and buy drugs from you...
Or if you teach those squares how to use their sex toys right...
They will always judge you...

CLYDE HURLSTON

But in the back of their minds they know...
That you hold all of their secrets... And yet you're still happy...
That's why they hate you...
You know why they hate me?
It's because I know that there is no God.
I'm just trying to inspire you to live like it...
'Cause I am...

WHEN AM I A MAN?

When am I a man?
That is the question you must first understand
Before finding the answer you've begun to seek
When the knowledge can be comprehended before I begin to speak
When are fantasies as real as they can seem?
Is it the nights when I infiltrate your dreams?
Can I compose your happiness today?
A song and smile to be sent your way
When do the birds sing upon your windowsill?
Is it when you lie awake in our bed so still?
When can the words good morning dance across your face?
Like when you missed our hello kiss, and can still drink its taste
When can you feel a look more than a touch?
When nothing is said and that alone is too much
Is it when you whisper to me of your request?
When to fulfill a wish I do my best?
But there will be days when your friends envy us
As their support gives way to such hateful lust
They long to feel the passion burns
With which we brand our hearts as this planet turns
It is true, my actions at time can be abrasive
But your touch is calming, and yet so persuasive
God knows best for me, and that my dear is true
Am I the blind man lost, within the parameters of you
Memories guide my way, and helped me to find today
But I asked a question first, so this is what I have to say
When am I a man?
Or more importantly when did I become a man?
Was it the day I was given the gift of life from the Lord above me?
Yes that could be,
But baby I believe I became a man,
On the day you first said you love me.

ECSTASY

Ecstasy, far from some little colored pill
But an honest to God thrill
That I get when you make that sound, of joy abound
As if signaling to the Heavens
The arrival of a god into the parameters of your being
Of which for me, cannot rival seeing
That sparkle in your eyes,
As I drift slowly beneath your navel
Which somehow makes me able
To speak in tongues with my tongue
Words that only your other pair of lips can understand
Which causes painted nails to dig into my skin
Like the way the roots of trees penetrate the sand
And oh my do I, love the way you shiver, the way you quiver
Like somehow the temperature has dropped
My ego inflates as you gasp, like a child
When their new balloon has unexpectedly popped
And because you taste like water from a spring, and with your tongue
You can do that one certain thing
It makes me wanna drop down to one knee, and give to you a ring
Filled with diamonds,
Whose beauty cannot hold a candle to your own
But under the candlelight, you are divine,
In the moonlight, you are a goddess
And if I can be honest, I am so glad that you are mine
But nothing can match the feeling that I get,
From seeing you get wet
With sweat, mind you
After a night of giving me your all, after I have given you mine
You should really hurry and get dressed, or you'll be late for work
Babe, I'm serious, just take a look at the time
But wait, one last thing before you go
You asked me what is ecstasy
It's being able to put my hands, my lips, and my fingertips
On any and every part of you
Because I know that you truly love me
And yes my dear, I do love you too.

DEMENTIA

In my darkness may your triumphs find light
In my wrongs may your realize the things that are right
In my soul lies a pain that shall acquiesce to your touch
In my heart there is thought of you hurting me much
Do you smirk at my intuition? Do you deny such logic?
Do you wish to deplete my mind? While keeping for yourself it's profit
Are you cold-hearted? Do we share that emotion?
Do you wish me to suffer? Or do you bring to me devotion?
Will you give me your love, and all the things I ask?
Or am I too overwhelming? And is that too great a task?
Speak to me in your native tongue, and I'll respond without words
Take my heart and soul at once, like a shepard's gathered herds
But there I dare to glance and say, they come with a lofty price
With my love comes vengeance, please choose to heed this advice
Love me and do me wrong, I'll follow you to Gates of Hell
Brand you with my Scarlet Letter, and wish you wear it well
Why are my thoughts so dark, is what you often wonder
It's because I've been drowned in light, and the sun's shine never reaches under
Under the weight of the pain, I've placed on myself
Collecting dust is the Bible, that lies upon the shelf
That displays that picture of you, the one my eyes can't bare to see
In remembrance of things you did, to prove your lack of care for me
I wish it not to be this way, but it's how I've always been
Even when this life was well, my outlook was steady grim
I know not who to blame, so I'll blame the one I hate
The one who I see inside this looking glass, the keeper of my fate
But this person's not in focus, seems the glass won't let me see
The one who it is I hate,
But now it seems I can, and alas the one I hate is me...

CLYDE HURLSTON

FLY WITHOUT WINGS

In your eyes, I find
The answer to life's greatest question
And what I do with the knowledge
Is left up to my discretion
Lightning flashes, in an instant
A surge of emotions is all I feel
I have to keep pinching myself
To prove to me that you are real
To truly love, is what we all yearn to do
Just have faith in me, I'll show you this much is true
Thinking of you my love, and all of the joy it brings
To truly live, is to fly, to fly without wings
Dreaming while awake
Baby, just let your emotions guide you
And I feel reborn
Everytime you allow my love inside you
I'm a mirror of a man
I reflect everything that you give to me
And everyday I shall thank the Lord for you
His precious gift to me
To truly love, is what we all yearn to do
Just have faith in me, I'll show you this much is true
Thinking of you my love, and all of the joy it brings
To truly live, is to fly, to fly without wings
Soaring amongst the Gods, your love takes a man to new heights
While I'm loving you throughout the longest days,
And throughout these endless nights
You make me feel, like alive, is the greatest thing to be
So baby please, don't ever take your love away from me
To truly be loved, is what we all yearn to do
Just have faith in me, I'll show you this much is true
Thinking of you my love, and all of the joy it brings
To be with you, is to fly, to fly without wings

THE DANCE

In our minds we share a dance
And on the floor we find the fear to give our love a chance
With swords and knives, it's our thoughts we guard
And to deliver fear a killing stroke has become as hard
As it is to fly inside a fleeting summer's breeze
When our ship has been troubled in all the seven seas
But when dancing, they say you should never lead with your left
And I look at the life I lead, and wonder what I have left
For the world isn't very kind
When your reality doesn't fit the image in their mind
Remember that they'll disregard your hopes and dreams
And only focus on the brands and sizes of your jeans
It's a photogenic world, full of plastic people with morals for sale
And they'll include a tan in a bottle, in case you're feeling a little pale
Paint your eyelashes black, so we won't notice your eyes are always shut
And pay your surgeons well, so they'll remove every self-inflicted cut
In our souls we share a dance
And on the floor we find enough guilt to give religion a chance
With swords and knives, it's our beliefs we guard
And to deliver sin a killing stroke has become as hard
As it is to devote ourselves to something we cannot see
While reading about miracles performed by a man we'll never be
But when dancing, they say the more experienced one should lead
And still the timid take control, because it's our egos we love to feed
For the gossip of sinners isn't very kind
When they're searching lives with fine-tooth combs, for what they'll never find
And remember that they'll disregard the truth, if lies bring more delight
It's not about who are you today, but what you do at night
And they love to know who you do it with, and details make them smile
They show their teeth to throw you off, their second face is just as vile
Paint your windows black, so they can see a reflection of their hearts
And they'll know their lives won't equal yours, unless they combine the parts

CLYDE HURLSTON

FLY INSIDE A BROKEN SKY

As the stars fall into place
I sit down and picture your smile
The way it glowed upon your face
I drown in my memories for awhile
As planets chase the sun
I pretend that these aren't tears I cry
But when all is said and done
To suppress this pain, I must still try
And I know, that you can fly
Because I watched you fly away
And although, I don't know why
I feel like I'm gonna die today
As the children laugh and play
I suffocate the thought of you
Couldn't find the words to say
After what you put me through
And as eagles soar, my sky looks black
Clouds spit their hate on me
Lightning flashes, as thunder cracks
Seems happiness couldn't wait on me
And I know, that you can fly
Because I watched you fly away
And although, I don't know why
I feel like I'm gonna die today
And I know, that you really lack a heart
Because you torn mine from the very chest
As your silence tears my soul apart
I guess I'll just fade away like all the rest
And yet, you pretend that you don't hear me
Don't know what I'd do, if you were near me
Probably scream or threaten
Because my hate seems to be my only weapon
And I know, that you can fly
Because I watched you fly away
And although, I don't know why
I feel like I'm gonna die today
And I know, that you really lack a heart

BROKEN SKY

Because you torn mine from the very chest
As your silence tears my soul apart
I guess I'll just fade away like all the rest

IN YOUR ARMS

When I think of you
I picture a devil with horns
Once a beautiful rose
In my heart you inserted your thorns
Then you drained me of life
Moved on to research
And since you look down on me
I'll scream up to your perch
Being inside of your arms
Is like a nail through the palms
Then you'll cast me to the side
Just to hide what's inside
What have I done to deserve
To receive this hate you preserve
There's only one thing I know
And it's that one of us has got to go
When I look in your eyes
I see the culmination of lust
On a canvas without color
Like ashes without all the dust
Then you stare back into mine
Now tell me what do you see
Could it be you've run out of time
Or has guilt been blinding you to me
Being inside of your arms
Is like a nail through the palms
Then you'll cast me to the side
Just to hide what's inside
What have I done to deserve
To receive this hate you preserve
There's only one thing I know
And it's that one of us has got to go
Nail to me to the wall, display me with pride
Let the world see what you did, til I dried up and died
Then I'd come back again,
See you through the holes in my palms
And not feel at home, until I was back in your arms

BROKEN SKY

Being inside of your arms
Is like a nail through the palms
Then you'll cast me to the side
Just to hide what's inside
What have I done to deserve
To receive this hate you preserve
There's only one thing I know
You might be the one, of us, that's got to go

CLYDE HURLSTON

BELIEVE

When you, look deeply within
Do you see past, the color of skin
And everytime, you speak aloud
Should I get the feeling you're proud
To see through a different set of eyes
Will you keep reaching for your prize
Will you walk alone, or create your own path
And can you embrace, the aftermath
I believe there's something in you
That makes you like me
And if that's true
Do you hit your knees nightly?
I believe that if you give thanks
Everything will fall into place
Just let me hold you closely
And wipe the tears from your face
The time has come, there you go trusting again
Hush now, because I know how it's been
You put your trust in someone
Who will just turn around, take it, and run
Fear not, 'cause karma's coming for them
Best known to us, as the repercussion of sin
And as sure, as He looks down from above
My hate for this world, is beginning to outweigh my love
I believe there's something in me
That turns you away
And you'll just keep walking
No matter the words that I say
I believe that if you turn your back on me
You've turned your back on yourself
This darkness I'm holding inside
Can't be good for my health
This world is so dark,
When viewed through my eyes
Inside the mirror,
Is the man I despise
Then you pull me close

BROKEN SKY

Do you feel my hate
Your love is a prison
And your chains I will break
This world is so dark,
When viewed through my eyes
Inside the mirror,
Is the man I despise
Then you pull me close
Do you feel my hate
Your love is a prison
And your chains I will break
I believe there's something in me
That turns you away
And you'll just keep walking
No matter the words that I say
I believe that if you turn your back on me
You've turned your back on yourself
This darkness I'm holding inside
Can't be good for my health

A SOUL'S ASYLUM

I hear knock on my door
A sound that I've come to abhor
A sight that I see,
Reveals that it's my past behind this glass
Please unbuckle this white coat
Remove your hands from my throat
As I fight to breathe,
Memories come flooding in so fast
Should I succumb to the pain
Or should I call out in vain
For a God that makes mistakes
I've been labeled insane
Medication's clouded my brain
And my spirit is what it breaks
Hands of time are still moving slow
TV's repeating the same tired show
The warden walks in,
Slaps me in the face,
And my own blood is what i taste
What kind of place is this
The brochure sold me bliss
The demons they laugh,
The sound filling the space,
It's what I wish I could erase
Should I succumb to the pain
Or should I call out in vain
For a God that makes mistakes
I've been labeled insane
Medication's clouded my brain
And my spirit is what it breaks
I'm fading again
My soul crumbles within
Dear God, it's of you I ask
Don't leave me here to die
I'd rather fly through the sky
Please place redemption within my grasp
Should I succumb to the pain

BROKEN SKY

Or should I call out in vain
For a God that makes mistakes
I've been labeled insane
Medication's clouded my brain
And my spirit is what it breaks
I don't care what they told me!
Padded walls will not hold me!
The world will not embrace me!
So God, you now have to face me!
I'm fading again
My soul crumbles within
Dear God, it's of you I ask
Don't leave me here to die
I'd rather fly through the sky
Please place redemption within my grasp...

CLYDE HURLSTON

GRASS IS GREENER

What did you do to your hair
Who picked out the clothes that you wear
Earrings are hanging too low
Was that how much cleavage you wanted to show
Critique your every move,
Why do you cater to them
Run you into the ground
Yet you still wish to befriend
This is a song, about a girl who is lost
Selling her soul, unaware of the cost
Wants to fit in, just follows the crowd
She hates herself, but never says it aloud
Never match your lipstick and shirt
That's way too long of a skirt
Your make-up is looking too rough
When will enough be enough
Come back to reality
You've been gone for too long
Your friends are so shallow
Acceptance won't help you be strong
This is a song, about a girl who is lost
Selling her soul, unaware of the cost
Wants to fit in, just follows the crowd
She hates herself, but never says it aloud
To me she's perfect, in every sense of the word
But she's a sheep, lost inside of the herd
I'm a shoulder to lean on, try to help her make sense
But I guess the grass is greener, on that side of the fence
Wolves in designer clothing, no see-through disguise
You're too blinded to see, you won't open your eyes
You're slipping away, I feel you losing your grasp
Spiraling downward, baby you're sinking so fast
Reach out for my hand, you're running out of time
To move on with your life, or get to the back of the line
They'll never care about you, they'll just cast you aside
Everything you ever need, I'll be here to provide
This is a song, about a girl who is lost

BROKEN SKY

Selling her soul, unaware of the cost
Wants to fit in, just follows the crowd
She hates herself, but never says it aloud
To me she's perfect, in every sense of the word
But she's a sheep, lost inside of the herd
I'm a shoulder to lean on, try to help her make sense
But I guess the grass is greener, on that side of the fence

PRICELESS ADVICE

This little masquerade of yours
Has to end
Secrets hidden behind the doors
Sins to defend
Hollow is what you've become
Face the lies
Question what have you done
Now that my trust has died
Remove the wool from across my eyes
Easier said than done
Deceitful and pretentious
There's nowhere you can run
Never far behind you
Your past will consume
Just admit to dishonesty
Then maybe this love can resume
You don't have to say a word
The truth said to me
When every ounce of what I felt
Is now dead to me
Showed me your true colors girl
The second face you wear
The blatant disregard
Is something I cannot bare
Remove the wool from across my eyes
Easier said than done
Deceitful and pretentious
There's nowhere you can run
Never far behind you
Your past will consume
Just admit to dishonesty
Then maybe this love can resume
Heartbroken, is now how I lay
Into the darkest night, you've flown away
And as I sit here, trying to keep my eyes dry
I'll never wonder, or bother to ask you why
Remove the wool from across my eyes

BROKEN SKY

Easier said than done
Deceitful and pretentious
There's nowhere you can run
Never far behind you
Your past will consume
Chased away by dishonesty
Now karma's gonna see you soon...

CLYDE HURLSTON

SIX FEET DOWN

Constant diet, force fed lies
Unwashed hands, pry open eyes
Bitter tongues, lash out of hateful mouths
The moaning grows, such awful sounds
Tortured souls, journey to the depths
Of your mind, willing to see what's left
What will they find, what do they seek
Maybe they'll rest, when you no longer speak
Six feet down, looking up at you
The shovel is there, you know what to do
Bury me alive, underneath your wall of doubt
And as I scream and cry, please refuse to let me out
Took everything, I once had to give
Now I don't know, if I deserve to live
Foolish man, who loved a whorish girl
Brought an end, to my fucking world
Was I too nice, or was I not nice enough
The dirt falls into place, you know I like it rough
Blinded from the start, could not begin to see
No rest for the weary, you're coming in with me
Six feet down, looking up at you
The shovel is there, you know what to do
Bury me alive, underneath your wall of doubt
And as I scream and cry, please refuse to let me out
Six feet up, looking down at you
The shovel is here, I know what to do
Bury you alive, now that the table has turned
There's no mercy bitch, your bridge has been burned
There is no punishment, for what you did
Loved me eternally, who are you trying to kid
As darkness closes in, make one last request
Just one last lie, for my heart to digest
Six feet up, looking down at you
The shovel's here, I know what to do
Bury you alive, now that the table has turned
There's no mercy bitch, your bridge has been burned
Six feet down, looking up at you

BROKEN SKY

The shovel is there, you know what to do
Bury me alive, underneath your wall of doubt
And as I scream and cry, please refuse to let me out

CLYDE HURLSTON

TEMPTATION'S TASTE

Bitter souls grace empty tombs
As lost kids dress their wounds
Stubborn ones swim against the tides
Embracing faith that it provides
The Lord smiles upon you now
Wipe the sweat from off your brow
Judgment saved for another's eyes
Wash away such dirty lies
Heaven can be found within your fingertips
Temptation's taste upon your lips
And if the way you feel, really is a sin
Let me inside, to be born again
Children play as parents scream
Demons flee as angels dream
I know not how to paint a scene
Only you can make me feel serene
Savor the chance to tell you this
Journey through hell to feel your bliss
As I fall unto my knees
Just kiss me girl I beg you please
Heaven can be found within your fingertips
Temptation's taste upon your lips
And if the way you feel really is a sin
Let me inside, to be born again
Hell is life, without your touch
So save me now, if it's not too much
To ask, from you my savior
I thank you Lord, because you gave me her
Stained glass, shines down with colors bright
The warmest smile, radiates throughout the night
Girl I long to hear, you call my name
Leave with me, upon the cloud I came
Heaven can be found within your fingertips
Temptation's taste upon your lips
And if the way you feel really is a sin
Let me inside, to be born again
Hell is life, without your touch

BROKEN SKY

So save me now, if it's not too much
To ask, from you my savior
I thank you Lord, because you gave me her

CLYDE HURLSTON

SCIENTIFIC APPROACH

As the volume increases, our temperatures rise
An inferno rages inside, the both of our eyes
You hypothesize, what I will do next
Usually ends up, with hands around each other's necks
Remember when, you used to fantasize and dream
Now it's been replaced, with a stiff kick and a scream
So I think you should know, how this chapter will close
We'll have our emotions, remain all juxtaposed
Let's use the scientific approach
To figure out, why we're always at each other's throats
Night after night, this shit's getting old
I think it's time, for us to release the hold
Dreams disperse, the same way most vapors do
A Dear John letter, yes I read those papers too
Our love has dissolved, as you sit and you stare
Cloaked in mistrust, my how well you wear
Your heart, the abyss enclosed in your chest
Dysfunctional, is a word that describes us best
Now that perfection, has been depleted today
In the ashes of love, I must find my way
Let's use the scientific approach
To figure out, why we're always at each other's throats
Night after night, this shit's getting old
I think it's time, for us to release the hold
The hold, that we have on each other's hearts
The one that leaves egos bruised, and battered counterparts
Remnants of you, still stain my skin
Along with my tainted heart, you wish to consume again
The world's biggest words, can't describe how I feel
I'll slap me for you, proving this pain is so real
You desire the accolades, when all you deserve is the blame
And mark my words, you shall not forget my name
Let's use the scientific approach
To figure out, why we're always at each other's throats
Night after night, this shit's getting old
I think it's time, for us to release the hold
The hold, that we have on each other's hearts

BROKEN SKY

The one that leaves egos bruised, and battered counterparts
Remnants of you, still stain my skin
Along with my tainted heart, you wish to consume again

CLYDE HURLSTON

THE GIFT OF LIFE (HEADS)

Eye a sight so desolate
Yes this is the best you'll get
Unless you start to appreciate
The time it takes for you to wait
For God to unleash His grace
An angel's tears fall upon your face
As the clouds manipulate the Earth
Show Satan how much you're worth
Would you live or die
Would you smile or cry
Would you take my hand
Could you understand
That we've all been given a gift
To help our souls finally lift
It's dangerous, like the blade of a knife
And all it is, is the gift of life
Escape into the wilderness
Scrape away your bitterness
Worn so proud upon your sleeve
All your heart does is grieve
What makes you keep your distances
Missing precious instances
If I could remove your veil of doubt
I'd show you how to live without
Would you live or die
Would you smile or cry
Would you take my hand
Could you understand
That we've all been given a gift
To help our souls finally lift
It's dangerous, like the blade of a knife
And all it is, is the gift of life
Nothing compares, to the air that I breathe
And it would escape me again, by watching you leave
So promise you'll stay, until night turns into day
Appreciate life together, it's really the only way
Would you live or die

BROKEN SKY

Would you smile or cry
Would you take my hand
Could you understand
That we've all been given a gift
To help our souls finally lift
It's dangerous, like the blade of a knife
And all it is, is the gift of life

CLYDE HURLSTON

THE GOSPEL ACCORDING TO…

Trample on your faith
Middle finger toward the sky
Spit in the face of God
Answer as I ask you why
Why do you hate the one
That paid all of your debts
And burrow into my decency
All without a hint of regrets
Now the time has come
For you to answer for
Taking everything I am
Plus just a little more
As judgment is handed down
I ask was it worth it
To be broken down
Revealing your circle's far from perfect
Stick me with your unforgiving tongue
Words like spears fly inside my heart
Apology, no I never expected one
Soon as I rise, you take the central part
What have I done to you
To make you act this way
Heed all the words I sing
'Cause you're gonna get yours one day
Now the time has come
For you to answer for
Taking everything I am
Plus just a little more
As judgment is handed down
I ask was it worth it
To be broken down
Revealing your circle's far from perfect
Fires shall burn your skin, who'll be beside you then
As you look for assistance, they'll be gone like the wind
I'll be right here waiting, for you to extend your hand
As I turn my back, maybe then you will understand
Now the time has come

BROKEN SKY

For you to answer for
Taking everything I am
Plus just a little more
As judgment is handed down
I ask was it worth it
To be broken down
Revealing your circle's far from perfect

CLYDE HURLSTON

PERFECT LITTLE DRUG

Let the attacks on me commence
The irony, being that you're not making sense
Possibilities are fading fast
In the race to save your decency, you're falling into last
Pushing the very limits of what you think
It can be over, just as fast as you can blink
If you want my help, baby just ask for it
I feed off your helplessness, I honestly adore it
This time, there'll be no games you play with me
This time, I'll just let you have your way with me
When you're bad, oh fuck it feels so good
So good I'd sell you to the world, if only I could
When will you understand
That only you can hold me in the palm of your hand
And when will you comprehend
That you'll be on your knees, when the day comes to an end
And I'll be there, to take advantage of your need
For me, your lips are saturated by your greed
One kiss, can take this situation to higher heights
And nothing gets us off, like our nightly fights
This time, there'll be no games you play with me
This time, I'll just let you have your way with me
When you're bad, oh fuck it feels so good
So good I'd sell you to the world, if only I could
So we could all, taste you and get high
Absorb your energy, and never question why
So come to me now, satisfy my craving
And it'll be this world, that you end up saving
Just one more touch, just one more sip
I need you here, won't you help me get a grip
One more taste, and I'll watch you climax
Just get undressed, so the world can get off our backs
This time, there'll be no games you play with me
This time, I'll just let you have your way with me
When you're bad, oh fuck it feels so good
So good I'd sell you to the world, if only I could
So we could all, taste you and get high

BROKEN SKY

Absorb your energy, and never question why
So come to me now, satisfy my craving
And it'll be this world, that you end up saving
You're my perfect little drug.
You taste so good.
You're my perfect little drug.
My time, you waste so good.
You're my perfect little drug.
You feel so good.
You're my perfect little drug!
Oh God, you heal so good!

CLYDE HURLSTON

WHAT'S A MAN TO DO?

I sat down this morning
My first thought is of you
And outside it is storming
Keep thinking what should I do
My cell phone's on the table
And oh, I want to call
But it seems I'm unable
If I'm too eager I'll lose it all
What's a man to do
When he can't stop thinking of you
And it seems like he's falling fast
Feelings should not be rushed
Or his heart will get crushed
Because we know nice guys finish last
But with you I feel different
You get me high
They tell me I'm foolish
But I don't know why
Is there something in your past
That I should beware
A movie with a revolving cast
I think if you kiss me again, I will not care
What's a man to do
When he can't stop thinking of you
And it seems like he's falling fast
Feelings should not be rushed
Or his heart will get crushed
Because we know nice guys finish last
Throw caution into the wind, just to see you again
I can't describe, how I'm feeling within
I'll give you my heart, just take care of it girl
Stay by my side, and I will try to give you the world
They tell me I'm foolish
And that you're wrong for me
But then I heard you say:
"Boy, sing that song for me..."
What's a man to do

BROKEN SKY

When he can't stop thinking of you
And it seems like he's falling fast
Feelings should not be rushed
Or his heart will get crushed
Because we know nice guys finish last
What's a man to do
When he can't stop thinking of you
And they keep telling me what I should know
They will pray that we'll fail
And our ship will never set sail
So they can say I told you so...

WISH YOU THE BEST

I, have something to confess
Something to get from off my chest
It's the only way I will feel relief
Oh and I, can't deny it any longer
Because the pain is getting stronger
Spent my days stricken by guilt and grief
I wish you all the best
For the reason's what you'll ask me
Girl, I just wanna see you happy
Even if it's not with me
I wish you all the best
I'll just stay here and remember
This was my coldest December
Because you're not with me
I, caused our relationship to demise
Went searching and I already had my prize
How could I screw things up this bad
Oh and I, miss the way you kissed my lips girl
Feeling your skin on my fingertips girl
I threw away, the best thing I ever had
I wish you all the best
For the reason's what you'll ask me
Girl, I just wanna see you happy
Even if it's not with me
Girl, when I look into your eyes
I see the reflection of my lies
And that alone, will haunt me forever
I wish there was something I could say
To take the things I've done away
Then maybe we'd, still be together
I wish you all the best
For the reason's what you'll ask me
Girl, I just wanna see you happy
Even if it's not with me...

A SOUL UNDER CONSTRUCTION

The ashes of our love
Lay scattered about
Broken lights flash above
The person I can't do without
The light reflects in her eyes
But it's blinding to me
It's tough to get through my lies
That's what she's starting to see
The walls that I've built
Are often held up by guilt
Of the things I never did
You want me to wear
A cross I can no longer bear
Oh, who am I trying to kid
The pieces of our life
Lay shattered below
Sharp like blade of a knife
I shouldn't touch them I know
But I can't help to feel
Regret for all of her pain
Wounds unable to heal
Now she wants me to hurt her again
The walls that I've built
Are often held up by guilt
Of the things I never did
You want me to wear
A cross I can no longer bear
Oh, who am I trying to kid
Our broken hearts, have become equal parts
In the ignition of our self-destruction
Those caught in the blast, will remember the past
I'm just a soul, that's under construction
The walls that I've built
Are often held up by guilt
Of the things I never did
You want me to wear
A cross I can no longer bear

CLYDE HURLSTON

Oh, who am I trying to kid
Yes, the walls that I've built
Are often held up by guilt
Of the things I should not regret
You want me to wear
A cross I can no longer bear
Oh, how could you forget?

AMONGST THE COMMON FOLK

I told her she's a goddess
But she's behaving rather modest
All of the boys bow down in respect
She's mad 'cause every single courtship
Somehow turns into a worship
So humility forces her to neglect
But we put her atop a high horse
Our actions are taking their course
The other girls don't have half of her class
Now she's mad 'cause every man's appointment
Ends with disappointment
Yet half full remains her view of the glass
Even though I'm not the one for her
I still continue wanting her
'Cause I long to see that look in her eyes
Everyday I'm thinking maybe
She'll start to call me baby
And then I can cash in on her prize
She and I had a conversation
About the devastation
She tends to bring to all of their lives
On herself she lays the blame
Her hands hide her face in shame
She's looking for pleasure, they're looking for wives
But she's got the magic touch
That makes it hard to get enough
Especially when she whispers a request in your ear
She'll leave you caught up in a reverie
You better cherish every memory
Roll over in the morning, and she's no longer there
Even though I'm not the one for her
I still continue wanting her
'Cause I long to see that look in her eyes
Everyday I'm thinking maybe
She'll start to call me baby
And then I can cash in on her prize
Darling, life amongst the common folk,

CLYDE HURLSTON

Is so hard for you
But with the gift you possess,
What else can you do
Don't try pleasing others,
Worry about pleasing yourself
And if you think you're changing her,
You're only teasing yourself
And even though I'm not the one for her
I still continue wanting her
'Cause I long to see that look in her eyes
Everyday I'm thinking maybe
She'll start to call me baby
And then I can cash in on her prize
Why can't you see?
I'm on my knees girl...

BLANKET OF LOVE

Insults are hurled
Aimed straight at your self-esteem
You think they're righteous
So their actions you redeem
Do you walk blindly
Into the direction of their voice
Or are you finding
That discretion is your choice
Hush, you're safe now
From the world that lurks above
So tattoo your hate
Onto the blanket of my love
Now you're put on display
Like a puppet for this world to view
Hear me when I say
Don't let them get the best of you
Dancing on their strings
Can't sever any of the ties that bind
Fathom the pain it brings
To have the knife inserted from behind
Hush, you're safe now
From the world that lurks above
So tattoo your hate
Onto the blanket of my love
Who will you run to,
When you find that you've been betrayed
Where will you run to,
When you see the path that I have blazed
Who will hold you,
And mend the pieces of your heart
It's like I told you,
I've been here from the very start
Hush, you're safe now
From the world that lurks above
So tattoo your hate
Onto the blanket of my love
Baby, tattoo your hate

CLYDE HURLSTON

Onto this world that's caused you pain
While I penetrate your heart
And watch the love pour down like rain...

EMBRACE THE NIGHT

People pass by inside their cars
I look up and the night is crying stars
I sit and wonder where you are
But my journey would not take me far
I saw you with another man
Holding what seemed to be another hand
I felt the internal crumble of my trust
I've been humbled by one who caved in to lust
I can barely form the words
To express the things I feel
Love is just a mere facade
Pain the only constant real
If I could say one thing to you
After what you've put me through
I'd say thanks for being so far from right
You inspired me to embrace the night
As you kissed him my stomach turned
The fire inside increased its burn
Then you somehow saw me there
As his fingers ran through your hair
He didn't not see as we locked eyes
You read my face and felt despised
I don't why you began to cry
As you let another fool find comfort in your lies
Now I can barely form the words
To express the things I feel
Love is just a mere facade
Pain the only constant real
If I could say one thing to you
After what you've put me through
I'd say thanks for being so far from right
You inspired me to embrace the night
Why must we resist
Though no one enjoys feeling like this
I know not what to say
But I think it's better this way
Because I no longer fight myself

CLYDE HURLSTON

Paranoia's not good for my health
So now I'll finally end this fight
Accept the destiny of embracing the night
Because I can barely form the words
To express the things I feel
Love is just a mere facade
Pain the only constant real
If I could say one thing to you
After what you've put me through
I'd say thanks for being so far from right
You inspired me to embrace the night
Yeah, after all is said and done
The night is the only thing that holds me tight.

FIRST TO LAST

How can I say what I feel
Without sounding redundant
How can I make you see
That I'm everything he wasn't
I have never raised my voice
I have never raised my hand
But you don't seem to rejoice
You just try to understand
Why do you keep questioning
When the answers are in front your face
Why is your silence deafening
I think it's time for a change of pace
If I've said it once
I've said it a million times
You're all I wish to see
Everytime I open my eyes
But we can't move forward
Until you let go of the past
'Cause I may not be your first
But I swear that I will be your last
How can I show you
That these are way more than words
Or do you feel like a sheep
Thinking I'm the wolf amidst the herds
Why can't you see
That I'm everything I ever said I'd be
No hidden agendas
What you see is what you get with me
Why do you keep questioning
When the answers are in front your face
Why is your silence deafening
I think it's time for a change of pace
If I've said it once
I've said it a million times
You're all I wish to see
Everytime I open my eyes
But we can't move forward

CLYDE HURLSTON

Until you let go of the past
'Cause I may not be your first
But I swear that I will be your last
Why can't you see
That I'm everything I ever said I'd be
Baby, open your eyes!
What you see is what you get with me
If I've said it once
I've said it a million times
You're all I wish to see
Everytime I open my eyes
But we can't move forward
Until you let go of the past
'Cause I may not be your first
But I swear that I will be your last...

HERE IT IS

I'd journey through hell
Just to feel your kiss
Recount the stories I'd tell
Just to feel like this
I can't look away
From a sight so divine
I'd go to the ends of the Earth
Just to make you mine
You belong to me
That's what I believe
Said sing a song to me
You asked and received
Here it is
I fulfilled your request
And it yours to keep
That which beats in my chest
Do what you please
Keep it or cast it away
Just tell me of your love
And I'll believe what you say
I'd journey to a land filled with ice
To feel your warmest embrace
Even in a world without lights
My eyes could outline your face
Because I know it so well
I think I dreamed you to life
Girl you keep me on edge
Let's dance on the blade of the knife
You belong to me
That's what I believe
Said sing a song to me
You asked and received
Here it is
I fulfilled your request
And it yours to keep
That which beats in my chest
Do what you please

CLYDE HURLSTON

Keep it or cast it away
Just tell me of your love
And I'll believe what you say
Is this what you want, is this what you need
I'm confessing my love, you've yet to take heed
Why must you make, me sit here and wait
Save me from myself, I'm overloaded with hate
You belong to me
That's what I believe
Said sing a song to me
You asked and received
Here it is
I fulfilled your request
And it yours to keep
That which beats in my chest
Do what you please
Keep it or cast it away
Just tell me of your love
And I'll believe what you say...

IN THE MORNING I'LL MOURN

The moon shows itself again
Signaling the departure of today
And I just look deep within
But I can't find the words to say
Because they told me you're gone
Up there amongst the angels now
And I just look up and smile
Because I know you're looking down
And this song I sing, it came to me
While thinking of the love you gave to me
I dream of you, each and every night
Ever since the day you saw the light
And this song I sing, I sing for you
Because your memory, helps pull me through
To see, every morning's light
I won't mourn until then, in your name I rejoice tonight
The night continues passing by
Oh my how the time does fly
I wonder where do the days go
As I remember all of our good times
It seems as if it were yesterday
That you were here by my side
And although you may have died
You're forever alive, alive inside of me
And this song I sing, it came to me
While thinking of the love you gave to me
I dream of you, each and every night
Ever since the day you saw the light
And this song I sing, I sing for you
Because your memory, helps pull me through
To see, every morning's light
I won't mourn until then, in your name I rejoice tonight
As I sing to Kevin, to Chris and to Shawn
Your memories will still live on
To Grandpa and every Uncle that has passed
My love for you will always last
And this song I sing, it came to me

CLYDE HURLSTON

While thinking of the love you gave to me
I dream of you, each and every night
Ever since the day you saw the light
And this song I sing, I sing for you
Because your memory, helps pull me through
To see, every morning's light
I won't mourn until then, in your name I rejoice tonight!

LISTEN TO YOUR HEART (TAILS)

Eye a sight so desolate
Yes this is the best you'll get
Unless you start to appreciate
The time it takes for you to wait
For God to unleash His grace
An angel's tears fall upon your face
As the clouds manipulate the Earth
Show Satan just how much you're worth
Although this world will misguide you
The things you need, are buried deep inside you
Just do, what needed to be done from the start
Close your eyes, and listen to your heart
Escape into the wilderness
Scrape away your bitterness
Worn so proud upon your sleeve
All your heart does is grieve
What makes you keep your distances
Missing precious instances
If I could remove your veil of doubt
I'd show you how to live without
For although this world will misguide you
The things you need, are buried deep inside you
Just do, what needed to be done from the start
Close your eyes, and listen to your heart
Although this world will try to change you
Break you down, and then rearrange you
Just find comfort in, the words that I've said
Then let your heart wear the crown, and not your head
In this world, judgment comes swift and fast
And separated, we will not last
The time is now, let's come together
If not we'll, just fall forever
I know that our souls are ill
So won't you dry those tears you spill
Because love's a pain that is so real
Look into my eyes, find what you need to heal...
Although this world will misguide you

CLYDE HURLSTON

The things you need, are buried deep inside you
Just do, what needed to be done from the start
Close your eyes, and listen to your heart
Although this world will try to change you
Break you down, and then rearrange you
Just find comfort in, the words that I've said
Then let your heart wear the crown, and not your head!

LIVING PUZZLE

It's been an eternity
Since my life's been run by fear
As my pen hits this page
It's met with a falling tear
The tears leave a trail
Blazing their way down my face
And without you in my life
Girl, I feel so out of place
The man I wish to be
Would never feel this way
And the woman I wish to love
Would never walk away
The man I wish to be
Would be the man inside your dreams
But the truth is I'm a puzzle
Falling apart at his seams
It's felt like forever
Since my pieces fit together
I bet that she could save me
If only I'd break down and let her
Could you make it all complete
Without your patience wearing thin
If frustrated is how you felt
Feel free to start all over again
The man I wish to be
Would never feel this way
And the woman I wish to love
Would never walk away
The man I wish to be
Would be the man inside your dreams
But the truth is I'm a puzzle
Falling apart at his seams
I never meant to push away,
The one that brightened up my day
Now the clouds have turned black and gray
And I cannot find the words to say
So baby please return to me,

CLYDE HURLSTON

You're the lesson I've learned indeed
Can't you see that I'm in dire need,
Of your love to resume completing me
The man I wish to be
Would never feel this way
And the woman I wish to love
Would never walk away
The man I wish to be
Would be the man inside your dreams
But the truth is I'm a puzzle
Falling apart at his seams
Yes, I'm a living puzzle
That's far too mixed-up...
And falling apart at the seams.

MEDIEVAL THOUGHTS, MODERN MIND

It's in my world
That pleasure's never lasting
My soul hungers for you
Because it's been here fasting
In this kingdom of mine
I have been searching to find
Someone to end my isolation
In this land of desolation
Will you be there
To fit beneath my arm just right
Will you promise me
You'll never disappear at night
Will you be there
To witness every breath I take
Will you promise me
You'll be here when I wake
Today I'll visit my magician
Ask him to cast me a spell
I'll give him your description
And tell him to conjure it well
Because lonely and desperate
Are much too far from separate
This has been one constant nightmare
So I'll keep wishing from right here
Will you be there
To fit beneath my arm just right
Will you promise me
You'll never disappear at night
Will you be there
To witness every breath I take
Will you promise me
You'll be here when I wake
What I didn't know was bad news was lurking
He said, "Son, my spell isn't working."
This isn't an attempt to taunt you
But this girl may already want you
If your heart is in the right place

CLYDE HURLSTON

Just look her right in her face
And repeat everything you told me
And maybe, just maybe she will hold thee
...for the rest of your life
Darling, will you be there
To fit beneath my arm just right
Will you promise me
You'll never disappear at night
Will you be there
To witness every breath I take
Will you promise me
You'll be here when I wake?

MY PHILOSOPHY

Who knew you could make something simple
Out of something that's complex
You're not finished with today
And still you look forward to the next
How can you be so free at heart
When the world's coming to an end
That's when you turned and looked and said
Let me tell you how my friend
You just close your eyes
And face the breeze
As your worries melt
With the greatest of ease
It's my own philosophy
To never let it get me down
Because there is so much to see
When you stop and look around
As I stood there my mouth was open
And all you could do was smile
To feel these feelings is what I'm hoping
Because it's been awhile
Since I could lay my head at night
And not toss and turn or fight
With memories of a dreadful past
'Cause in the race of life I used to finish last
You just close your eyes
And face the breeze
As your worries melt
With the greatest of ease
It's my own philosophy
To never let it get me down
Because there is so much to see
When you stop and look around
A wise girl said to stop and smell the roses
Grab a camera and strike your poses
Live your life like tomorrow's not guaranteed
And I said that's what I should have done
To escape a past I can't outrun

CLYDE HURLSTON

In case you missed the point, this is what I mean
You just close your eyes
And face the breeze
As your worries melt
With the greatest of ease
It's my own philosophy
To never let it get me down
Because there is so much to see
When you stop and look around...

SHOULD HAVE WENT

In the light of day
Things seem so much clearer
Why do I look away
From what I see in the mirror
I don't know why
I can't be at peace with myself
But I won't cry
Because I don't receive any help
I'll stand up on my own two feet
Rise above setbacks and defeat
This day head on is what I will meet
And try remove this taste so bittersweet
I'm just a normal man
Trying to do the things I can
To make this life worth living
Reclaim the gifts I've been giving
To the ungrateful people that I adore
I give until there's nothing more
Than regrets and time well spent
This is how my life should have went
I make believe you understand
Why I say things so profound
My life is like a written plan
But I still stop and look around
I don't smell flowers or wish on stars
I just love you and your mistakes
Even though I don't know where you are
I hear your heart when it breaks
Stand up on your own two feet
Rise above setbacks and defeat
Name a place where we can meet
To make our lives feel complete
I'm just a normal man
Trying to do the things I can
To make this life worth living
Reclaim the gifts I've been giving
To the ungrateful people that I adore

CLYDE HURLSTON

I give until there's nothing more
Than regrets and time well spent
This is how my life should have went
Name a place where we can meet
To make our lives feel complete
This day head on is what we will meet
No longer does life taste so bittersweet
Because I'm just a normal man
Trying to do the things I can
To make this life worth living
Reclaim the gifts I've been giving
To the ungrateful people that I adore
I give until there's nothing more
Than regrets and time well spent
This is how my life should have went

SHOW ME YOUR WORLD

Mountains feel like velvet
As they reach for the sky
Demeanors are often melted
When they're seen by the naked eye
And I journey onward
Through this uncharted land
So much can be learned
Through the touch of my hand
From your highest high
To your lowest low
You have so many things
That you can show
I'm willing to learn
If you're willing to teach
Just show me your world
And I'll speak without speech
And now a valley lays hidden
So pure is the taste
Of the fruit considered forbidden
That I sample with haste
These waters run so free
As the landscape begins to dance
Oh, what sights these eyes do see
While caught inside this euphoric trance
From your highest high
To your lowest low
You have so many things
That you can show
I'm willing to learn
If you're willing to teach
Just show me your world
And I'll speak without speech
This exotic location,
Is truly a secret
Knowledge is power,
How long can you keep it
If you answered forever,

CLYDE HURLSTON

Then I will tell you the truth
Welcome to Heaven,
You can bathe in this fountain of youth
Baby, from your highest high
To your lowest low
You have so many things
That you can show
And I'm always willing to learn
If you're willing to teach
Just show me your world
And for you, and you alone,
I will speak without speech.

SWEETER SIDE OF HEARTBREAK

You know these milk chocolate minds
Are often filled with malice
As you tumble down the rabbit hole
To reunite with your friend Alice
And down there is a crazy cat
That proudly displays his grin
Fawning over the chewy center
That you hide within
How I love to taste,
These candy-coated lies
'Cause the truth tastes better,
When it's in disguise
We have flavors like mint,
To help freshen your breath
And mask our love's decay,
While inhaling the smell of this death
You know these candy canes are red
With their stripes of white
Think because you taste so good
That it somehow makes it right
And now it seems to me
That I can finally understand
Why you melt inside my mouth
But never in my hand
But still I love to taste,
These candy-coated lies
'Cause the truth tastes better,
When it's in disguise
We have flavors like mint,
To help freshen your breath
And mask our love's decay,
While inhaling the smell of this death
They say what goes up,
Must come back down,
Follow those yellow bricks,
Buried in the ground
Follow that blazen trail,

CLYDE HURLSTON

Until you make it home
Because your mouth stays dry,
The longer you're alone
Unless you've learned to love the taste,
Of these candy-coated lies
'Cause the truth tastes better,
When it's in disguise
And we still have flavors like mint,
To help freshen your breath
And mask our love's decay,
While inhaling the smell of this death
Yes, it will mask our love's decay
While leaving proof of our death...

BROKEN SKY

UNDERNEATH THE AUTUMN SUN

As the leaves and their colors change
Your brown eyes stay the same
Are we more than lovers
Or is there another name
For what we have become
Underneath the autumn sun
There are ways of describing this
And here is my favorite one
The leaves are fallin' for me
Because they do adore me
I know you hear me callin' for thee
So baby, please don't ignore me
And when it comes to love,
You need to start anew
Because the leaves fall for me my dear
But not as slowly as you do
'Cause when the world is turning cold
Girl I have a hand that you can hold
And together we'll face the day
And we'll let the leaves fall where they may
Sitting on a park bench patiently
Waiting on your every word
And then I had a daydream
That I had finally heard
"Baby, you know I love you
And I'll place no one above you
So please stand up and turn around
And just let me hug you"
The leaves are fallin' for me
Because they do adore me
I know you hear me callin' for thee
So baby, please don't ignore me
And when it comes to love,
You need to start anew
Because the leaves fall for me my dear
But not as slowly as you do
'Cause when the world is turning cold

CLYDE HURLSTON

Girl I have a hand that you can hold
And together we'll face the day
And we'll let the leaves fall where they may...
Keats said, "Truth is beauty, and beauty is truth"
Just as imagination is the basis of youth
Young and vibrant she came to me
At a time when autumn and winter looked the same to me
The colors once bright turned dark to sight
Just as day is sure to give way to night
She passed not fast, and bestowed a glance
Her eyes met mine, as if by chance
A gift from God, the spark ignites
The stars they shine, like steady lights
They guide my thoughts, as they begin to race
I close my eyes, the dark outlines her face
I have fought to feel, these emotions pure
A welcomed disorder, I seek no cure
If my love for you, will be the death of me
Girl I leave for you, what is left of me
And yes my dear we will go on
Because our love is far from gone
Although work puts me in another place
Not a day goes by that can erase
Who you are and what you've meant to me
Because I feel that we were meant to be
Girl, to your love I remain a slave
Until I lay flowers down upon your grave...
So when the world is turning cold
Girl I have a hand that you can hold
And together we will face the day
But 'til then, let the leaves fall where they may
Can't you see the leaves are fallin' for me
Because they do adore me
I know you hear me callin' for thee
So baby, please don't ignore me
For when it comes to love,
You need to start anew
Because the leaves fall for me my dear
But not as slowly as you do.

A SONG FOR MARY

There's a distance between right and wrong
Like attraction between both word and song
Light courts darkness, so the dark will seek light
And if you think I'm wrong, does that make you right
What's that, you're not making any sense
Has the girl unchained thoughts, by using false pretense
Because on her reason, you used to choke
Now you have foresight, to guide you through the smoke
This is an ode, to the respect she's been owed
By those whom undress her of covers, becoming her lovers
This world can be scary, so i beg you be wary
Then do us a favor, and please sing this for Mary…
And now this girl sells her soul, in measurements of fun
Dangerous, everytime pleasure vents the gun
Whether an ounce or a gram, who truly gives a damn
She'll blow your mind, just say thank you ma'am
Driving you crazy, is it she behind the wheel
Do you need her kiss, to truly make you feel
Like, the world is cold and without soul
Drowning in misery, in this city that's shaped like a bowl
This is an ode, to the respect she's been owed
By those whom undress her of covers, becoming her lovers
This world can be scary, so i beg you be wary
Then do us a favor, and please sing this for Mary…
So controlling!
She makes you keep rolling!
Nevermind what they've said!
Just take her to your head!
Breathe her in, blow her out!
And then let her know…
What your love is all about!
This is an ode, to the respect she's been owed
By those whom undress her of covers, becoming her lovers
This world can be scary, so i beg you be wary
Then do us a favor, and please sing this for Mary…

THE ART OF SIMPLICITY

A blank piece of paper
Floats through an autumn wind
No one's there to witness
The occurrence of this my friend
This page just flips and tumbles
Unsure of where it will land
I search for meaning in its journey
And then I finally understand
We have much in common with this page
Floating unknown through this day and age
And then the picture is drawn
Not a bishop or pawn
But a king searching for his queen
Follow the bleeding trail of ink
To understand the thoughts I think
And find the underlying theme
Now I'm sitting on a bench
A million different cars pass me by
Exhaust leaves a familiar stench
Yet the birds do their best to fly
And the nosy trees hide their bend
They want to read the words I write
Then a stranger wishes to pretend
That there is no danger in the fall of night
And then the picture is drawn
Not a bishop or pawn
But a king searching for his queen
Follow the bleeding trail of ink
To understand the thoughts I think
And find the underlying theme
These sights are not enough
Because I haven't seen a woman's love
Except from my mother's hands
And like an hourglass
They can't even hold the sands
And now the sun is finally going down
It leaves its' stain on a deceitful town

BROKEN SKY

I live here, and leave here
But I don't make it very far
Because here is where you are
And then the picture is drawn
Not a bishop or pawn
But a king searching for his queen
Follow the bleeding trail of ink
To understand the thoughts I think
And find the underlying theme
That asks: "Girl, where are you?"

ASHES OF DECENCY

You are the martyr for me
The symbol of all that I've lost
Crucify what you believe
Nail my soul to a cross
Drive a stake through my hand
If I reach out for you
Make this world understand
Proceed to preach of my doom
Since I don't care what you want
I don't care what you need
I'm in the grips of the demons
I have to focus to feed
I'm drowning in sin, and you paint me a saint
I'm destroying myself, and I won't file a complaint
You say I can be saved, but it seems to me
You're sifting through, the ashes of my decency
Don't label me a pagan
Though I blaspheme at times
All debts have been paid
I'm absolved of my crimes
Sentenced myself to a life
Without the warmth of embrace
I pushed away my love
So I could get another taste
And I don't care what you want
I don't care what you need
I'm in the grips of the demons
I have to focus to feed
I'm drowning in sin, and you paint me a saint
I'm destroying myself, and I won't file a complaint
You say I can be saved, but it seems to me
You're sifting through, the ashes of my decency
I don't care, how often you pray
Only one thing, can take my pain away
Wrap me in chains, the grips of withdrawal
I've failed you before, now watch as I fall
I don't care what you want

BROKEN SKY

I don't care what you need
I'm in the grips of the demons
I have to focus to feed
I'm drowning in sin, and you paint me a saint
I'm destroying myself, and I won't file a complaint
You say I can be saved, but it seems to me
You're sifting through, the ashes of my decency
Yes, you're sifting through the ashes of my decency...
You're sifting through the ashes of my decency...
To be more frank, you're sifting through,
The memory of the man I was!!

CLYDE HURLSTON

ARMAGEDDON COME EARLY

Know not the pastor
That shall flock the most wayward of sheep
Know not these brown eyes
That shall close while refusing to weep
Know not just the Father
But His Son, and the Holy Ghost
Yet will you know me
After all, I'm just your party host
My friend, open your eyes
And help us penetrate the minds
Of those who can't think for themselves
Just know we'll be treated unkind
When they come to find
They keep a book of lies on top of the shelves
Know not just the woman
Who's name was betrayed for thousands of years
Know the man who died
Ground soaked from his blood and all of her tears
Know not just the hands
Pierced with the stakes for the sins of us all
Know he who understands
That truth is Almighty, and soon the false churches will fall
My friend, open your eyes
And help us penetrate the minds
Of those who can't think for themselves
Just know we'll be treated unkind
When they come to find
They keep a book of lies on top of the shelves
If this world is going to end
Why must keep trying to pretend
That this is something, we will be able to stop
Let's just live it up, until the day the bomb finally drops
Will you spend your time
On a church pew preparing to tithe
Knowledge needs no reason or rhyme
But to believe is to define the word of alive
My friend, open your eyes

BROKEN SKY

And help us penetrate the minds
Of those who can't think for themselves
Just know we'll be treated unkind
When they come to find
They keep a book of lies on top of the shelves...

CLYDE HURLSTON

BEHAVIORAL ANALYSIS

With behavior so ostentatious
Do you expect an ovation
When everything you say
Gets repeated inside of quotations
And yet here I am
Foolishly remaining humble
With your actions designed
To make any ego crumble
I try my best,
To close my eyes and look away
Look for a sign,
Or any shade of brighter day
But there's no hope for me,
Caught in the same games you play
And silence begins to rape,
The nice things that we used to say
With behavior so passive
How can I expect to get respect
When I'm pushed to the side
Force fed a spoonful of neglect
Yes this jagged little pill
Is often swallowed whole
As I feel the hate for myself
Burning deep within my soul
I try my best,
To close my eyes and look away
Look for a sign,
Or any shade of brighter day
But there's no hope for me,
Caught in the same games you play
And silence begins to rape,
The nice things that we used to say
You try your best to coax,
A confession of affection
But it remains a hoax,
Thrust me into the grips of rejection
Then go bragging to your friends,

BROKEN SKY

that I'm subservient to you
Am I beneath your finger's end,
Oh, the shit you put me through
I try my best,
To close my eyes and look away
Look for a sign,
Or any shade of brighter day
But there's no hope for me,
Caught in the same games you play
And silence begins to rape,
The nice things that we used to say

CLYDE HURLSTON

BLEEDING IN PLAIN SIGHT

A wise man once said
To be or not to be
But I should've asked
When it's okay to bleed
Because I've poured out my heart
So you'd taste the overflow
And embrace what you've made
When the stains decided to show
Why'd you take the stitches out so soon
Like you were prepared to dress this wound
Instead you watch as the blood begins to pool
Oh my, how the red glows beneath the moon
My pain's escaped again
Will you ignore it tonight
It's hard, to hide in shame
When you've been bleeding out in plain sight
This pool of blood
Mirrors when we first met
Seems it was a sign
Of my impending regret
The second stain
Is my favorite one
Let's see if you recall why
When this is said and done
Why'd you take the stitches out so soon
Like you were prepared to dress this wound
Instead you watch as the blood begins to pool
Oh my, how the red glows beneath the moon
My pain's escaped again
Will you ignore it tonight
It's hard, to hide in shame
When you've been bleeding out, in plain sight

BRAND NEW YEAR

Birds are flying overhead
They spell out the words you've said
So I stop to read them all
And it's a request for me to crawl
Back to you, right back to you...
Sorry, but I've been down that road before
And I don't wanna travel anymore...
The birds have left my view
The same way that I did to you
Broken glass in the picture frame
A shot of me, next to one without a name
I have forgotten, you should do the same...
Sorry, but I've been down that road before
And I don't wanna travel anymore
So I'll just stand right here, erase my fear
And look forward to this brand new year
The birds are heading south
Away from the things that come out your mouth
You had the world, and chose to discard
So now I hold you, in my lowest regard
Sorry, but I've been down that road before
And I don't wanna travel anymore
So I'll just stand right here, erase my fear
And look forward to this brand new year
I wish you good luck rebuilding
With the tidal waves your eyes keep spilling...

COLORS

Some colors are light
But my favorites are dark
Because they mostly reflect
The current state of my heart
Images often get replayed
Inside my thoughts at night
As the neon begins to fade
And the colors start to blur just right
There'll be a day when you come to find
The colors aren't profound anymore
When you keep your heart under locks
But you can't seem to close Pandora's Box
The brightest shade of red
Is coursing through my veins
The darkest shade of gray
Mirrors the clouds when it rains
But who do you run to in life
Do they embrace you with open arms
Are their words gravitational
Do you fall victim to foolish charms
There'll be a day when you come to find
The colors aren't profound anymore
When you keep your heart under locks
But you can't seem to close Pandora's Box
The overwhelming burden of guilt
Threatening to destroy all that we have built
Rumors fuel our inferno's flame
True colors show revealing our shame
But today I've come to find
The colors aren't profound anymore
When they can kill what we were
But not the memory of what we stood for
There'll be a day when you come to find
The colors aren't profound anymore
When you keep your heart under locks
But you can't seem to close Pandora's Box...

COULD I BE?

Could I be the high heels,
That you just bought
I'm like sex in public,
A rush until you get caught
There's a thought that's been haunting
Could I be the dolphin,
Swimming through your right hand
Maybe even the rabbit,
Asleep inside your nightstand
It's something that I've been wanting
There's no limit to what I could be
But you keep saying what I should be
You're waiting for, what destiny may never bring
For the love of you, I could be your everything
Could I be the opinion,
You live your life by
Could I be that movie,
That makes your eyes cry
To ask if I could be the one thing
Could I be a painting,
Posted on your wall
Instead of the number,
You wrote down but never call
That will someday mean something
There's no limit to what I could be
But you keep saying what I should be
You're waiting for, what destiny may never bring
For the love of you, I could be your everything
There's a thought that's been haunting
It's something that I've been wanting to do
To ask if I could be the one thing
That will someday mean something to you
Am I just the white stain,
On your bedsheets
Something you need,
When you try to be discreet...
Could I be the gold ring

CLYDE HURLSTON

On your left hand,
Probably not
Seems like you'll never understand...
There's no limit to what I could be
But you keep saying what I should be
You're waiting for, what destiny may never bring
For the love of you, I could be your everything.

BREAKING AWAY

Sometimes I wonder
If the weight that I'm under
Will bring me to the ground
But if I lay tired
With my strength expired
Will I even make a sound
Maybe I'm like the tree that's fallen
I don't know if you'll hear me calling
But I still have to try
Because maybe you'll one day save me
With the love that you gave me
Or will you just leave me here to die
But I'm still breaking away from yesterday
So please heed the words I say
I'm so tired of this daily monotony
Time to look forward to brighter days
And really fight to change my ways
'Cause look how far the old way's gotten me
Am I broken completely
Could you rebuild me discreetly
Or are the pieces too small
I know that it's not right
Just blame it on the height
From your grace, I took a nasty fall
Maybe I'm like the tree that's fallen
I don't know if you'll hear me calling
But I still have to try
Because maybe you'll one day save me
With the love that you gave me
Or will you just leave me here to die
But I'm still breaking away from yesterday
So please heed the words I say
I'm so tired of this daily monotony
Time to look forward to brighter days
And really fight to change my ways
'Cause look how far the old way's gotten me
People tell me, it's not that bad

But they know nothing of, the life I've had
That's the reason they don't cry...
But maybe I'm like the tree that's fallen
And I don't know if you'll hear me calling
Yet I still have to try...
But I'm still breaking away from yesterday
So please heed the words I say
I'm so tired of this daily monotony
Time to look forward to brighter days
And really fight to change my ways
'Cause look how far the old way's gotten me...

COMFORT IN SUFFERING

It's been months
Since sunlight has touched my face
And It's been years
Since I've felt the warmth of embrace
But how can you miss me
If I've never been gone
And how can you love me
If you've just led me on
Why should I come out today
When I prefer the cold of night
If I find beauty in darkness
Why should I lean toward the light
I love this loneliness
The silence brings me comfort
And the reason why is I
Have suffered enough hurt
Now are you mad
At these points that I have raised
Or that you never had
The attention I give to those I praised
When you get off on thanks
Like you've been saving lives
When you've done nothing
But continue raping mines
Why should I come out today
When I prefer the cold of night
If I find beauty in darkness
Why should I lean toward the light
I love this loneliness
The silence brings me comfort
And the reason why is I
Have suffered enough hurt
Now I'm feeling tipsy
I've swallowed intoxicating lies
You profess that you miss me
Why does this come as a surprise
That I would say fuck you

CLYDE HURLSTON

You really could not foresee
That I'd say fuck you for every nothing
You ever did for me
Why should I come out today
When I prefer the cold of night
If I find beauty in darkness
Why should I lean toward the light
I love this loneliness
The silence brings me comfort
And the reason why is I
Have suffered enough hurt...

COUNTERCULTURE

Things were much different
During the era of Panthers
Questions were asked
Until they were answered
Now fast forward a few years
Racism still lingers
While we just make excuses
And keep pointing our fingers
They say no one can see
The true feelings we hide
We act one way in public
And show another inside
We pretend that we're flawless
When our point of views are broken
And our children are mirrors
They reflect what we show them
Millions move forward
After two towers have fallen
Fear is an unwanted stranger
Who does his best to keep calling
Times keep on changing
While our leaders are clueless
These wounds are self-inflicted
Why on Earth would they do this
They say no one can see
The true feelings we hide
We act one way in public
And show another inside
We pretend that we're flawless
When our point of views are broken
And our children are mirrors
They reflect what we show them
Our culture pretends to be righteous
And only a few choose to fight this
Education is piss poor
We're still in the grips of this war
We've seen more devastating disasters

CLYDE HURLSTON

While the clock's ticking faster
Is doomsday now nearing
Or are we too busy fearing
They say no one can see
The true feelings we hide
We act one way in public
And show another inside
We pretend that we're flawless
When our point of views are broken
And our children are mirrors
They reflect what we show them.

CYBERNETIC WAYS

Her eyes are both so laser sharp
She's an angel missing both halo and harp
She's fresh off the assembly line
With the thought, that one day she will be mine
Now they engage and proceed to caress
They say her skin is shiny and cold
When information cannot process
That means this captor's finally taken hold
This imitation of life
Is navigating the night
Looking for a man she can own
Until she leaves him alone
Her body's built to perfection
Which brings me to this question
Where on Earth is her soul?
Her cybernetic ways are out of control
Her body's covered with all sorts of gadgets
Her fragrance attracts men like magnets
Even the strongest become weak
When they inhale the words that she speaks
I sit back and watch her lure a victim
I think to myself how does she pick them
Then I open my eyes to see
This soulless machine is approaching me
This imitation of life
Is navigating the night
Looking for a man she can own
Until she leaves him alone
Her body's built to perfection
Which brings me to this question
Where on Earth is her soul?
Her cybernetic ways are out of control
Now I'm running through this nightclub
To escape the grips of her love
It's too one-sided for me
And I can tell she's excited to be
On this chase for a soul to possess

CLYDE HURLSTON

How did I get inside of this mess
I stop in hopes of catching my breath
Oh shit she saw me...
I guess there's only a moment left
Because this imitation of life
Is navigating the night
Looking for a man she can own
Until she leaves him alone
Her body's built to perfection
Which brings me to this question
Where on Earth is her soul?
Her cybernetic ways are out of control...

THE DEFINITION OF PURPOSE

This is an ode to battles fought
On a battlefield of dreams
The culmination of random thought
Slowly seeping through the seams
Bound and gagged the silent smile
When no cares to speak or bleed
Inside they're laughing all the while
Their captors are starving
The mental beast they need to feed...
The purpose of showing
Answers to the all knowing
Is the conformation of truth
The purpose of scolding
The child that you're holding
Is the wrongful suppression of youth
When your tears begin to evaporate
Does that mean emotions have stopped flooding
Or is it that each eye has closed a gate
And left you feeling nothing
Well I'm more inclined to think of you
As the embodiment of porcelain
You're not so easy to see through
And you'll break if my love is forced within
The purpose of showing
Answers to the all knowing
Is the conformation of truth
The purpose of scolding
The child that you're holding
Is the wrongful suppression of youth
Flashes of visions
Arrive with precision
I rush to interpret them all
Left battered and broken
I'm thinking, you're choking
Your lungs are refusing to answer the call
Will you answer me?
When it comes to worlds...

CLYDE HURLSTON

Is your world serene
Is mine so really bleak
Do you ever mean
The words you speak?
The purpose of showing
Answers to the all knowing
Is the conformation of truth
The purpose of scolding
The child that you're holding
Is the wrongful suppression of youth...

DR. JEKYLL & MR. HYDE

There are things in this world
That make us turn away
Our eyes turn blind
To the sights of yesterday
We pretend we don't see
Things that happen to the ones we love
But we owe it to them
To extend a hand and pull them above
You love feeling secure
You love a man who will provide
So you try your best to justify
The pain you feel inside
And now you're drowning in love
Up to you neck in fear
Hugs get replaced by shoves
The ugly sounds you have to hear
Shades cover dark circles
While make-up hides bruises
Oh you walked into a door
Time to stop making excuses
You love feeling secure
You love a man who will provide
So you try your best to justify
The pain you feel inside
I don't want them to call me
And tell me you've died
Because you loved Dr. Jekyll
And didn't run from Mr. Hyde
You deserve to be treated,
Like you are a queen
And not like the star,
In this horror movie scene
You don't want to leave,
Afraid to live your life alone
But I swear I'll take his life,
Before I let him take your own
You love feeling secure

CLYDE HURLSTON

You love a man who will provide
So you try your best to justify
The pain you feel inside
I don't want them to call me
And tell me you've died
Because you loved Dr. Jekyll
And didn't run from Mr. Hyde...

DROWNING IN SORROW

As I stand,
Waiting on your shore
I begin to understand
You're not fond of life anymore
Waves start to crash,
I see that look in your eyes
And it seems like,
You're gonna capsize under all of your lies
Now you're drowning,
Inside your sorrow
Won't fight for today,
But will you fight tomorrow
Will you vanish,
Beneath the surface
And make me feel,
Like our love is worthless?
And it's now that you,
Want to extend your hand
After I tried,
Everything that I can
To pull you back,
From the edge of your vice
I fear now is the time,
That you pay for rejected advice
Now you're drowning,
Inside your sorrow
Won't fight for today,
But will you fight tomorrow
Will you vanish,
Beneath the surface
And make me feel,
Like our love is worthless?
I can fight for you,
If you won't fight for yourself
So tired of trying,
Of wiping the tears that I'm crying
No, you won't fight,

CLYDE HURLSTON

You'd rather stay there and die
And it's breaking my heart,
'Cause it's been that way from the start
Now you're drowning,
Inside your sorrow
Won't fight for today,
But will you fight tomorrow
Will you vanish,
Beneath the surface
And make me feel,
Like our love is worthless?

END OF ACT I

"People are interested in birds only in as much as they exhibit human behavior - greed and stupidity and anger - and by doing so, they free us from the unique sorrow of being human."

-Douglas Coupland

"Relationships are like birds. If you hold tightly, they die. If you hold loosely, they fly. But if you hold with care, they remain with you forever."

-Unknown

2
A SKY BETRAYED

"In the sky, there is no distinction of east and west; people create distinctions out of their own minds and then believe them to be true."

-Gautama Buddha

CLYDE HURLSTON

"RAINING DARKNESS"
ART BY VALISA BERNARDINO

EDGE OF INSANE

Your face is the inspiration
For a painting I once painted
About a world that is twisted
From a point of view that's tainted
But alas I've come to find
Your colors are running down the canvas
Your love, shackles for the mind
And I can't stand this
Release your hold!
Your grip is cold!
If you can't let go!
Then you should know!
I can't get the taste of you
From clinging to my lips
I can't get the feel of you
From stinging my fingertips
Where is there to run
When you're in the grips of such pain
The sunlight never comes
When you're on the edge of insane
Outline your self-corruption
While tracing your past mistakes
Erase your imperfections
Sweep away the mold that He breaks
You're a work of art
Put so proudly on display
But be careful, 'cause you're fragile
One tear can wash you away
Release your hold!
Your grip is cold!
If you can't let go!
Then you should know!
I can't get the taste of you
From clinging to my lips
I can't get the feel of you
From stinging my fingertips
Where is there to run

CLYDE HURLSTON

When you're in the grips of such pain
The sunlight never comes
When you're on the edge of insane
Exhibit one, release your hold!
Exhibit two, your grip is cold!
Exhibit three, you can't let go!
Why can't you see, that you should know!
I can't get the taste of you
From clinging to my lips
I can't get the feel of you
From stinging my fingertips
Where is there to run
When you're in the grips of such pain
The sunlight never comes
When you're on the edge of insane.

EMPOWERED BY CHOICE

We're living in a world
Where all things seem the same
And people are meaningless
If there's no money behind their name
The rich disregard the poor
'Cause they live above the law
But today that seemed to change
With the dreadful sights I saw
Standing silent, one man drew his gun
Caged by fear, they all turned to run
Just one blast, means lives will end
Tragedy, has struck again my friend
The next day a man found a map
With the destination marked
Fantasies of solid gold
So on a journey he embarked
And this man didn't heed
Tales of quicksand and ravines
Blinded by his growing greed
That was the last time he was seen
They pushed this man, far beyond return
Igniting the greed, that will forever burn
A witness said, they heard it in his voice
He was empowered, by his final choice
And there was a third man
Who slept on a bed of stone
His new home was beneath the bridge
And yes he slept alone
Everyone of the passersby
Looked at him like he was strange
And they rolled their windows up
When he approached them for some change
They pushed these men, far beyond return
Inspired by despair, now they're gonna learn
And a witness said, they heard it in every voice
They all were doomed, by their final choice...

CLYDE HURLSTON

ENSLAVED BY A MIND

There's a darkness that I'm living in
All my friends condemn me for giving in
My thoughts constrict the very life
I had, that's now overcome with the strife
That I feel inside of my heart
Of all, it's become my least favorite part
Part of a temple that I curse to this day
So tell me what else do I need to say
Besides...
I'm enslaved to a mind that cannot be mine
And I'm hoping to replace it with time
I've been living this way for so many years
Drowned by a past filled with so many tears
Please save me...
I'm a victim of my own thought process
Leaving my faith labeled as nonsense
Will my God have mercy upon me
Or will he just curse who I've come to be
Answers like love, for me out of reach
Sharing my pain through the gift of our speech
Broken in spirit, cursed in the flesh
So burn out the bad and decipher what's left
I'm enslaved to a mind that cannot be mine
And I'm hoping to replace it with time
I've been living this way for so many years
Drowned by a past filled with so many tears
If you figure out just who I am
Please tell me when I give a damn
Don't tell me if I'm still living this way
Save the knowledge for a better day
I'm enslaved to a mind that cannot be mine
And I'm hoping to replace it with time
I've been living this way for so many years
Drowned by a past filled with so many tears

EYES WIDE SHUT

When standing on mountains things seem limitless
Doubt often misses when reaching for a preemptive kiss
The masses come in herds to worship such a feat
Masquerading to keep their envy buried underneath
A layer lost to religions and their foolish ways
When disasters strikes they proclaim it's the end of days
If the world's ending will I see signs or will I hear lies
Can someone quell the cities burning inside my eyes
Children step right up, listen to my words
And rebel against, all these mindless herds
I refuse to be, one of the shepherd's sheep
With my eyes wide shut, until I'm laid to sleep
The preaching wolf, is now cloaked in wool
And across your eyes, is where he aims to pull
Take a sip of blood, dine on the body's bread
And before you know it, they're inside your head
Children step right up, listen to my words
And rebel against, all these mindless herds
I refuse to be, one of the shepherd's sheep
With my eyes wide shut, until I'm laid to sleep
My eyes are not wide shut!
Now my problem is not with God
But I despise His followers
Where is Mary Magdalene
The bible seems to have swallowed her
Often called a whore
Because she didn't know her place
So she disappeared from every page
Leaving not a trace
So Father tell me, am I the next to be erased?!
Children step right up, listen to my words
And rebel against, all these mindless herds
I refuse to be, one of the shepherd's sheep
With my eyes wide shut, until I'm laid to sleep
Because my eyes are not wide shut!
My eyes are not wide shut!
I say once again, my eyes are not wide shut!

GASOLINE LACE

There was a girl that was young and timid
Afraid of life and the rush of living
But at night she's often livid
Over the affection her husband isn't giving
She wants to let her hair down
But it's an act that seems so hard
That's because she was raised
And instilled with the fear of her God
But now she puts on
Her gasoline lace
Ignited by tears
That once streamed down her face
She tried to live right
And just got hurt in return
So now she just smiles
And visits the bridges that burn
She comes home from work a little early
Slips into something more revealing
Now she aims to please him surely
But irony has planned what he's concealing
She walks in and finds her husband with another
In the bed that they've been sharing
She strikes one match and drops the other
They run for their lives with sirens blaring
But now she puts on
Her gasoline lace
Ignited by tears
That once streamed down her face
She tried to live right
And just got hurt in return
So now she just smiles
And visits the bridges that burn
So now she's trying
Those so-called risky things
Like jumping out of airplanes
Just to test her wings
She swims with the sharks

BROKEN SKY

But she's not confined in a cage
She just rolls with the waves
In an ocean once filled with rage
But now she puts on
Her gasoline lace
Ignited by tears
That once streamed down her face
She tried to live right
And just got hurt in return
So now she just smiles
And remembers the bridges that burned.

GENESIS UPON US

I glance outside the windowpane
A shadow lays on the pavement
On a street once baron and plain
The sunlight makes a statement
It signals the arrival of a new day
What I do is left to my discretion
I have so many things to say
But there are so many questions
Has my destiny found me today
Is this the day I become what I'm supposed to be
Or will this day pass me by
Before I see what I'm supposed to see
Run if you can, crawl if you must
Since this genesis, is now upon us
Poisoned darts fly through the air
While I walk this path
I still proceed without a care
And victory is the aftermath
I challenge what's been done before
As I fight to make my mark
Just know that you can kill the dog
But you can't silence the echo of his bark
You can't resist what's been set in motion
On this fateful day
When others pledge their endless devotion
It is to you that we unite to say
Run if you can, crawl if you must
Since this genesis, is now upon us
Destiny has found me today
I've become who I'm supposed to be
We stand together under the sun
So listen as we sing as one
Run if you can, crawl if you must
Since this genesis is now upon us!

HARD-HEADED MAN

I get my stubborn ways from my father
And momma's the only one it seemed to bother
My brother always seemed to act the same
But we're all willing to accept the blame
I know sometimes I make you crazy
Because I come across as naive or lazy
I don't mean to seem that way
So this is all that I have to say
Last night we fought and you told me
This world won't stop until it's bought and sold me
And there we let it stand
There'll be days when I seem to know it all
Just please be there to catch me when I fall
Because I'm one hard-headed man
I don't know much in this cold and lonely world
I just know I can't live if you don't hold me girl
Mistakes are what I will often make
But to redeem myself I'll do whatever it takes
I would go to the ends of the Earth
Just to prove that I am truly worth
Every ounce of love you've given to me
Because a life without you, isn't really livin' to me
Last night we fought and you told me
This world won't stop until it's bought and sold me
And there we let it stand
There'll be days when I seem to know it all
Just please be there to catch me when I fall
Because I'm one hard-headed man
I'm sure there'll be days when I seem to know it all
Just please be there to catch me when I fall
'Cause if I hit the ground, I'm sure I'll break
And I'll regret the advice that I didn't take
Last night we fought and you told me
This world won't stop until it's bought and sold me
And there we let it stand
There'll be days when I seem to know it all
Just please be there to catch me when I fall

CLYDE HURLSTON

Because I'm one hard-headed man
I'm sure there'll be days when I seem to know it all
Just please be there to catch me when I fall
'Cause if I hit the ground, I'm sure I'll break
And I'll regret the advice that I didn't take...

HELL HATH NO FURY

She's bringing me down
My knees make love to the ground
I'm trying, to weather this storm
But her heart is torn, she's a woman scorned
A pretentious type of woman
She's a juryless judge
Condemning all my actions
While refusing to budge
Proudly beg for mercy
The words that she looked down and said
Like commandments sent from Heaven
They echo inside of my head
She's bringing me down
My knees make love to the ground
I'm trying, to weather this storm
But her heart is torn, she's a woman scorned
Now there's every indication
Emotions begin to rumble beneath
The long sought gift of vindication
Is hers alone to bequeath
A rib once described as wasted
Exchanged for fruit from her tree
Now that betrayal's what she's tasted
Witness what she's doing to me
She's bringing me down
My knees make love to the ground
I'm trying, to weather this storm
But her heart is torn, she's a woman scorned
It seems, redemption's out the question
As my fate, is left to her discretion
My heart lies bleeding through the hands
Of the only one, who understands
After everything I fought to preserve
Time to get what you deserve
She's bringing me down
My knees make love to the ground
I'm trying, to weather this storm
But her heart is torn,
She's a woman scorned...

HOPELESS

When you look into my eyes
Do you see me the way I do
When you hear the crack in my voice
Can you tell what I've been through
Everytime I'm out in public
Can you tell that I am so lonely
And everytime my wit has reached its' end
Why does no one ever come hold me
I've grown tired of living this way
There's nothing more I can say
So never question who wrote this!
Turn away like you did before
I can't put up with this anymore
You're the reason I feel so hopeless!
People tell me not to frown
Because someone may love my smile
But I'm a ship that's going down
Every second, another mile
There's no need for you to save me
Just ask the Lord to save yourself
And if I do happen to die
You have my permission to bury what is left
I've grown tired of living this way
There's nothing more I can say
So never question who wrote this!
Turn away like you did before
I can't put up with this anymore
You're the reason I feel so hopeless!
This has been said so many times
So many people have lost their minds
Over things done by those like you
The cause of the pain that we've been through
So if forgiveness is what you seek
Pay attention now as I speak
You can't give back what you stole from me
Now let me show you how cold I can be...
I've grown tired of living this way

BROKEN SKY

There's nothing more I can say
So never question who wrote this!
Turn away like you did before
I can't put up with this anymore
You're the reason I feel so hopeless!

I'D DO ANYTHING

Repairing the wounds
Left open to be seen
Stitch them up soon
Present them so clean
With salt-covered hands
The sting mirrors the pain
That not one understands
When three words are said in vain
I'd give anything
For just one day
To be spent around your way
I'd give anything
Just to hear you
And be near you again
Play me a tune
On the harp of your lies
On a hot day in June
The sun mirrors your eyes
Eyelashes are sun rays
You're still burning my skin
Summer brings me dark days
When you're not with me again
I'd give anything
For just one day
To be spent around your way
I'd give anything
Just to hear you
And be near you again
Look deep inside your mind
Have you finally come to find
That you can forsake me, you can replace me
But time itself could not erase me
From your memory…
I'd give anything
For just one day
To be spent around your way
I'd give anything
Just to hear you
And be near you again…

IMPROPER INTRODUCTION

Hello, I'm your conscience
The one that's not often consulted
When engaged in this nonsense
Which has often resulted
In your heart being worn
So proudly upon your sleeve
As another page is torn
Now you'll begin to grieve
Now here come the tears
Cried for the passing years
Has heartbreak made you humble
Now where will you decide to turn
As your hate begins to burn
Watch your dreams start to crumble
Hello, I'm your mind's eye
The one that's been kept from light
Just because it's not a lie
Doesn't mean he's always right
When will you come to see
Life through the sight of me
How much attention have you paid
Now that your soul is frayed
Now here come the tears
Cried for the passing years
Has heartbreak made you humble
Now where will you decide to turn
As your hate begins to burn
Watch your dreams start to crumble
Hello, I'm mister sweet and nice
Mister shoulder to lean on with unheeded advice
Goodbye, our hearts have yet to be introduced
But I ask you, really, what is the use
Now here come the tears
Cried for the passing years
Has heartbreak made you humble
Now where will you decide to turn
As your hate begins to burn
Watch your dreams start to crumble...

CLYDE HURLSTON

IN THE MIRROR

In the mirror there's a stranger
And I don't recognize him
His disposition is bitter
And his outlook is grim
What on Earth could make a man
Turn ice cold inside his heart
I asked if he was broken
He said no, he's just been torn apart
Then I said!
I try my best to keep away
From these games you love to play
Put my imperfections on display
So this is what I have to say
I'm not the best at what I do
But that's okay, because I am not you
I won't hide away in fear for years
As the sands of time fall like tears
I'll just do what I love to do
Not focus on what I've been through
As you keep wasting your mind
By trying to live your life through mine
In the mirror there's a stranger
And his looks are ugly at best
Because there's so much hatred
Weighing down the heart in his chest
The light just shies away
From the brown in his eyes
He wants to replace halos with thorns
And wear that crown until he dies
Then I said!
I try my best to keep away
From these games you love to play
Put my imperfections on display
So this is what I have to say
I'm not the best at what I do
But that's okay, because I am not you
I won't hide away in fear for years

BROKEN SKY

As the sands of time fall like tears
I'll just do what I love to do
Not focus on what I've been through
As you keep wasting your mind
By trying to live your life through mine
Daily battles and internal fights
Eternal thoughts through endless nights
Emotions war when he begins to think
That's when he proudly swings his sword of ink
Then I said!
I try my best to keep away
From these games you love to play
Put my imperfections on display
So this is what I have to say
I'm not the best at what I do
But that's okay, because I am not you
I won't hide away in fear for years
As the sands of time fall like tears
I'll just do what I love to do
Not focus on what I've been through
As you keep wasting your mind
By trying to live your life through mine

IN THE NAME OF GOD

They gather in a circle,
To pray and hold hands
There's an hourglass,
That's not catching the sands
The emperor patiently sits,
Inside his coliseum
He's ordered executions,
The masses are coming to see them
They're tossing hot coals
Under their iron chairs
The smell of burning flesh
And screams fill the air
Behind a wall of stone
The hungry lion awaits
Waiting on the signal
To open those gates
In the name of God
Horrors know no bounds
In the name of God
The churches release their hounds
Seek out the pagans
Bring me news of their deaths
In the name of God
Some breathe their last breaths
Fast forward now,
Away from the centuries past
You'll find a mindset
That somehow managed to last
The church has a face,
They've labeled him pope
To me he's just the noose
At the end of an invisible rope
He carved out his niche,
In Hitler's regime
Now he wears a rosary,
Claiming God's team
Who is he to wear,

BROKEN SKY

The clothes of reverence
Nations addicted to religion
A vision of dependence
In the name of God
Horrors know no bounds
In the name of God
The churches release their hounds
Seek out the pagans
Bring me news of their deaths
In the name of God
Some breathe their last breaths
Forgive me Father,
For today I have sinned
I've allowed them to see,
That I'm hollow within
They say they're absolved,
For their sins have been paid
So they engage in a cleansing,
That they call their crusades
In the name of God
Horrors know no bounds
In the name of God
The churches release their hounds
Seek out the pagans
Bring me news of their deaths
In the name of God
Some breathe their last breaths

JUSTIFY

This world is a place I wish to leave
Tired of wearing this broken heart on my sleeve
Although it is my favorite place to wear
This broken soul, has become my cross to bear
I'm being punished for crimes, I did not commit
And I can no longer put up with this shit
It's like staring down the barrel of a loaded gun
A shot in the dark has left me numb
As the world is staring down
Not a soul is caring how
My point of view has become so bleak
But they justify every word that I speak
They hit their knees, praying for deliverance
But then they succumb to their belligerence
Out of control, looking to feed every vice
Devouring sins, unaware of the price
They say pleasure comes at too great of a cost
But because I am who I am, they label me lost
Refuse to conform, which makes me a rebel by choice
Spit acid in the face, of those aiming to silence the voice
As the world is staring down
Not a soul is caring how
My point of view has become so bleak
But they justify every word that I speak
As the world is staring down
Not a soul is caring how
This world has become so fucked up
Is it really worth saving now?
Pretending they're righteous, what's buried beneath
The lies to which, they're turning their cheeks
They'll just judge me, because I live how I choose
And I've got the world to gain, with nothing to lose
As the world is staring down
Not a soul is caring how
My point of view has become so bleak
But they justify every word that I speak
As the world is staring down

BROKEN SKY

Not a soul is caring how
This world has become so fucked up
Is it really worth saving now?

CLYDE HURLSTON

THE LAST STEP

I opened the locked window
And then stepped outside
Closed my eyes, felt the wind blow
And swallowed all my pride
'Cause I have nothing left
But my health
And that's not enough
Why must this life be so rough
So I take that last step
And try to end it all
Let the cold Earth
Be there to catch me when I fall
There's no reason for
This life that I abhor
So as I take this one last breath
Please don't follow my last step
Life brought out the worst in man
Uncovered all my greed
And I'll never understand
Why I helped them with this deed
I've held this guilt too long
I know that I was wrong
So I can't outrun
The things that I have done
So I take that last step
And try to end it all
Let the cold Earth
Be there to catch me when I fall
There's no reason for
This life that I abhor
So as I take this one last breath
Please don't follow my last step
I spent my entire life,
Doing things I thought were right
And destroyed it all,
On that fateful night
Now it's almost time,

BROKEN SKY

Here's what I will say
Remember the places I have been,
And not the place where I will lay
So I take that last step
And try to end it all
Let the cold Earth
Be there to catch me when I fall
There's no reason for
This life that I abhor
So as I take this one last breath
Please don't follow my last step
Because I only took this step
Inside a hurting mind
I would never end it all
Because I've come to find
We have family and friends
Even if they number few
Who would be broken by
What our loss had put them through.

LIBERTINE DREAMS

As the black of night dissolves
The clouds slowly begin to race
Abused, the quiet Earth revolves
A mournful sun decides to give chase
Daylight melts the window panes
Your skin glows like morning skies
Overwhelmed by both our shames
Neither opens up their eyes
This is nothing more than a libertine dream
A place where reality is not what it may seem
Your fantasies may intervene
And paint for you such a blissful scene
The shining reflection of your new soul
Melts your well-made external facade
Revealing your one true goal
Enclosed in a quote from Marquis de Sade
As you both said, "Sex without pain
Is much like food without taste"
Reluctantly a smile will grace the face
Of the one who will cave in with haste
This is nothing more than a libertine dream
A place where reality is not what it may seem
Your fantasies may intervene
And paint for you such a blissful scene
But this dream doesn't last long
For your conscience is much too strong
I dream to be human without feelings of guilt
To break down the walls religions have built...
Look but don't touch
Touch but then don't drink
Is that asking for too much
For you to listen and not think
And to follow the straight path
Of the blind and unknowing
'Cause it is a sin to give in
To the appetite that will never stop growing...
This is nothing more than a libertine dream
A place where reality is not what it may seem
Your fantasies may intervene
And paint for you such a blissful scene.

LIBRARY OF LIES

In this story there's a mighty God
Who sacrificed His only son
Crucified, they believe He died
Until He rose again like the morning sun
They left His wounds unhealed
And in His tomb they left him sealed
But that hollow grave would never hold
The one sent to save my broken soul
As I turn another page
My heart's filling up with rage
Over stories tried and true
I don't know where to go, don't know what to do
In this story there's a pretty girl
Who's mad because I won't hold her
Says my actions drift between the extremes
Well my dear I guess I'm bipolar
I guess I'm just fucked in the head
Won't you come back to our bed
And give me a taste of your cure
Since the book says I have symptoms pure
As I turn another page
My heart's filling up with rage
Over stories tried and true
I don't know where to go, don't know what to do
As I turn another page
My heart's filling up with rage
Over the wool pulled across my eyes
Blinding me from this library built on their lies
Instead I hate, my fucking self
So take this book, place it back on the shelf
And you'll curse my soul, 'cause I won't read
This hallowed advice, I refuse to heed
As I turn another page
My heart's filling up with rage
Over stories tried and true
I don't know where to go, don't know what to do
As I turn another page
My heart's filling up with rage
Over the wool pulled across my eyes
Blinding me from this library built on their lies

ON THE SHORELINE

As a child they asked you
What you wanted to be,
When you reached this age
In the book of your life
It was the most important page
This was set in motion
Many moons ago
Grab the future, make it my own
And I won't let go
As I stand on this shoreline
I'm going to take what's mine
I shall stand on this shore
Nevermore
Chose to swim against the tide
Went headfirst into the waves
Confidence, what setbacks provide
Destroying the fear that enslaves
This was set in motion
Many moons ago
Grab the future, make it my own
And I won't let go
As I stand on this shoreline
I'm going to take what's mine
I shall stand on this shore
Nevermore
Grab the future and make it mine
This is the dawning of my time
As sure as the sun shines on top me
It would take God himself to try and stop me
This was set in motion
Many moons ago
Grab the future, make it my own
And I won't let go
As I stand on this shoreline
I'm going to take what's mine
I shall stand on this shore
Once and nevermore

PARENTS OF A REVOLUTION

Oh skylights
Can't repel the sun
So why fight
Or even try to rebel my son
He said mother, if we don't
Change the world who will
Even if it's my blood
That must spill
And they started marching
Into the town square
It was disheartening
What they found there
Oh Lord
Bless this boy with some sense
He acts on his own accord
Wants to die in a stranger's defense
He said father, are you blind
To the struggles that we face
Or are you against
Making here a better place
And they started marching
Into the town square
It was disheartening
What they found there
In a week they received word
But information came by mail
As his mother read
Her face slowly became pale
It said, "Mother
If this letter should
Reach you, it means I have died
And it's for the better good...
So just remember the boy
You once so proudly praised
And forget that he died for a flag
That never was raised...

CLYDE HURLSTON

PATRIOTIC BOX

The cars are driving slowly down the street
Moving like a pair of marching feet
Toward the most well-kept of our lawns
On this brand new day just after dawn
But a woman's here fighting back her tears
Thinking bout two decades worth of years
That she spent to raise the one
They'll lay to rest beneath the sun
The night before she had to choose
Which method that she would use
Would she have his casket open wide
Or would she hide her child inside
Maybe let the others see his gaping wounds
And hear every gasp within the room
But she chose to seal it tight
Because she could not bear the awful sight
They draped the flag across his coffin
The same one he saluted often
And now every night she cries
Wondering why her baby had to die
She can't wave goodbye to the sleeping
Because she's far too busy weeping
And thinking about the locks
On her son's patriotic box
Shots ring out inside the sky
As the soldiers say their goodbyes
She thinks about her son within the Earth
And wonders how much can this oil be worth
Then she was informed of her son's request
That she'd receive his military chest
When she got home she received the box
Watched her husband's tools break the locks
And they opened up the heavy lid
But now she wished she never did
As she hid her face within her hands
And now her husband understands
Why she feels so damn deceived

BROKEN SKY

When he sees the hundreds of letters never received
They draped the flag across his coffin
The same one he saluted often
And now every night she cries
Wondering why her baby had to die
She can't wave goodbye to the sleeping
Because she's far too busy weeping
And thinking about the locks
On her son's patriotic box..

PLEDGE NO ALLEGIANCE

Your ignorance is damning
Your thoughts into a stream
Instead of the ocean of wisdom
That should be your dreams
Have you become that blind
Or do opinions still blur the facts
When the hateful things you say
Can't be taken back
You plead your case for purity
While hoping to mask your insecurity
Your rhetoric is blasphemous
We pledge no allegiance, so quit asking us!
Are you alive
Or are you just breathing in
And will your children accept
The legacy of shame you're leaving them
You preach your beliefs
Safely behind your pulpit
Throw the brick and then hide your hands
So now who's the culprit
You plead your case for purity
While hoping to mask your insecurity
Your rhetoric is blasphemous
We pledge no allegiance, so quit asking us!
I never asked to be placed,
in this position
But I'm so tired of being,
Beaten into submission
Force fed the ideals,
Of those with one-track minds
They're not living the life,
So why can't I live mine
You plead your case for purity
While hoping to mask your insecurity
Your rhetoric is blasphemous
We pledge no allegiance, so quit asking us!

QUICKSAND

I try to talk
To those who don't understand
That my thoughts and confidence
Are stuck in this quicksand
And from my eyes
The world looks cold and pale
But I won't succeed
If I'm afraid to fail
The more I think, the more I sink
And no one here will pull me out
Drowned by words, almost submerged
I still have to open up my mouth
If I want to live
Then I have to sing
It's the saving grace
To which I cling
Attempts at redemption
Are often futile at best
Don't let me forget to mention
The tremendous weight inside my chest
From an overloaded heart
Pumping blood through unsuspecting veins
Test results are off the charts
No matter if it's only me that pains
The more I think, the more I sink
And no one here will pull me out
Drowned by words, almost submerged
I still have to open up my mouth
If I want to live
Then I have to sing
It's the saving grace
To which I cling
I have searched for words to say
That could truly describe the way
That I often feel inside
But it seems the words escape me
In a world that wants to forsake me

CLYDE HURLSTON

And just fuck with my pride
The more I think, the more I sink
And no one here will pull me out
Drowned by words, almost submerged
I still have to open up my mouth
If I want to live
Then I have to sing
It's the saving grace
To which I cling...

PRIDE

They say too much pride can kill a man
So I'm ready to die where I stand
Whether at the stake or a cross, we'll pay our cost
And enter this Paradise Lost
I possess a heart and a soul
Both at war with my mind
My hands are out of control
I'm too impatient to stand in line
The preacher gives a sip of wine
To one who's on the eleventh step
How is sin truly confined
On a road paved with our regret
They say too much pride can kill a man
So I'm ready to die where I stand
Whether at the stake or a cross, we'll pay our cost
And enter this Paradise Lost
Nowadays greatness is defined
But how many people you keep in fear
They just laugh and denounce the divine
And pull the crooked near
Everybody claims to be hardcore
Like they're one of those Goodfellas
But there's hasn't been a tougher man
Since they freed Mandela
They say too much pride can kill a man
So I'm ready to die where I stand
Whether at the stake or a cross, we'll pay our cost
And enter this Paradise Lost
They say too much pride can kill a man
Why is that so hard to understand
Pride and greed are the reasons blood will spill
Just like it did during the Massacre at Sharpeville
For Malcolm and Huey and Doctor King
This is the song I have chosen to sing
Even now they don't look within
They still focus on the color of skin
The only difference is now they hide

CLYDE HURLSTON

While keeping their hatred deep inside
I believe the dream you shared was true
So I guess it's a matter of time before they kill me too...
They say too much pride can kill a man
So I'm ready to die where I stand
Whether at the stake or a cross, we'll pay our cost
And enter this Paradise Lost.

THE PRICE FOR A LIFE

Step up to the auction block
Take a glance at the souls for sale
Watch the blue eyes turn blood red
And their tanned skin turn to pale
Painted nails crack and peel
As the blondest hair turns gray
And wise men no longer feel
The need to give their thoughts away
Enjoy your gifts, for as long as they last
The reality is, they'll be a thing of the past
What will you do, when the cheering stops
When no one remembers, the day your casket drops
Step up to the auction block
Look at the problems missing solutions
Here marriages last a couple of months
Yet they're labeled holy institutions
The only thing sacred in this place
Are the covers of magazines
Loyalty's an expensive accessory
When you patrol this shallow scene
Enjoy your gifts, for as long as they last
The reality is, they'll be a thing of the past
What will you do, when the cheering stops
When no one remembers, the day your casket drops
Enjoy your gifts, for as long as they last
The reality is, they'll be a thing of the past
What will you do, when your allure has faded
And you provoke the rage, of the public that's jaded
When the headlines read, you're no longer in need
Will you collapse, underneath the ego you feed
When your so-called friends, decide to neglect you again
To get back their love, how much will you spend
Enjoy your gifts, for as long as they last
The reality is, they'll be a thing of the past
What will you do, when the cheering stops
When no one remembers, the day your casket drops
Enjoy your gifts, for as long as they last

CLYDE HURLSTON

The reality is, they'll be a thing of the past
What will you do, when your allure has faded
And you provoke the rage, of the public that's jaded
Enjoy the limelight,
Enjoy your high life…
Fortune teller says despair's in your cards
So I'll leave you with my best regards…
Enjoy your gifts, for as long as they last
The reality is, they'll be a thing of the past
What will you do, when the cheering stops
When no one remembers, the day your casket drops

PRODUCT OF PAIN

This day is mine and,
The sun is shining
And my slaves are mining
Oh they dig, for just a few cents
And it makes no sense
You turn on your t.v,
But you don't see me
Because I'm good at hiding
For the things you wear
This is the cross they bear
We're a product of their pain
Yeah when it's out of sight
Then it's out of mind
But it's a product of their pain
Let's go to the shop now,
Where it don't stop now
If they don't sew, they get shot down
Children in the next room,
Dressed in their gloom
Hope they're reunited soon
Go through the proper channels,
If you can't handle
The fact that this story's true
For the things you wear
This is the cross they bear
We're a product of their pain
Yeah when it's out of sight
Then it's out of mind
But it's a product of their pain
For those in Sierra Leone
Who are on their own
I sing this for you
For those in the 3rd world
With stories unheard
I sing this for you
For the things you wear
This is the cross they bear

CLYDE HURLSTON

We're a product of their pain
Yeah when it's out of sight
Then it's out of mind
But it's a product of their pain
For those here at home
Who are on their own
I sing this for you
For those in the third world
With stories unheard
I sing this for you...

RELIGION IN THE RAIN

I step out into the street
Watch as the clouds begin to merge
Lightning reflects off wet concrete
Can you feel the powers surge
People shake as thunder screams
And the rain falls in fright
Vivid visions bring lucid dreams
My life has changed tonight
It's not hard to start anew
If you know what you have to do
And that's let the water wash away your pain
Then embrace the religion in the rain
I start to wonder if
The rain will really cleanse my sins
As another drop hits my face
I'll take a look within
At the man that I never was
And the man I'll forever be
Recalling the great things I've done
The things you never see
It's not hard to start anew
If you know what you have to do
And that's let the water wash away your pain
Then embrace the religion in the rain
For years I've waited
To feel rejuvenated
Is that day here
As I feel the angels' tears...
Can bad weather bring
Me, one simple thing
The chance to start again
And be reborn with a gust of wind
It's not hard to start anew
If you know what you have to do
And that's let the water wash away your pain
Then embrace the religion in the rain

CLYDE HURLSTON

SAND IN THE BREEZE

Back on the shore,
I see hills of sand
It's right then,
That I start to understand
That we're all like,
Sand in the breeze
Drifting endlessly,
With greatest of ease
Now the wind is picking up
Where it will take me, no one knows
Now the wind is kicking up
I will take you along, so hold me close
On a deserted city street,
Beneath the traveling feet
Of movers and shakers,
Is our journey complete
Have we found a spot to land,
Still hand in hand
Or have we forgotten
The destiny of the sand
Now the wind is picking up
Where it will take me, no one knows
Now the wind is kicking up
I will take you along, so hold me close
We are like sand in the breeze
We are like sand in the breeze
Drifting with the greatest of ease
We are like sand in the breeze
We are like sand in the breeze
Stay out of our way, won't you please
Now the wind is picking up
Where it will take me, no one knows
Now the wind is kicking up
I will take you along, so hold me close.

REMEMBER THE FORGOTTEN

I've been on a journey
Looking for someone to love
But alas I could not see
That sometimes to look is not enough
Because then you're blind
You follow your heart and not your mind
It's been this way for awhile
But no can see through this hollow smile
Life is the knife that's slicing my skin
Stabbing the love that I have buried within
Why is the only time, I am outspoken
Is the day, my heart gets broken
Life is the knife that's slicing my skin
Releasing the hate that I have buried within
Why is the only time, I am regretful
Is the day, you act forgetful
Now this journey resumes
One that I feel is futile
But God says that hate consumes
And despair is killing you my child
All you do is put down yourself
And that Book is collecting dust on your shelf
Pick it up so you can read
And let my wisdom finally plant its' seed
Life is the knife that's slicing my skin
Stabbing the love that I have buried within
Why is the only time, I am outspoken
Is the day, my heart gets broken
Life is the knife that's slicing my skin
Releasing the hate that I have buried within
Why is the only time, I am regretful
Is the day, you act forgetful
As you once gave your begotten seed
I swear that this world has forgotten me
All they do is pass me by
And I swear I don't know why
As you once gave your begotten seed

CLYDE HURLSTON

I swear that this world has forgotten me
All they do is pass me by
And I swear I don't know why
Life is the knife that's slicing my skin
Stabbing the love that I have buried within
Why is the only time, I am outspoken
Is the day, my heart gets broken
Life is the knife that's slicing my skin
Releasing the hate that I have buried within
Why is the only time, I am regretful
Is the day, you act forgetful...

SILHOUETTE OF SOMETHING MORE

Rest your soul on a bed
On a bed of rusted nails
While dreaming of dead men
Re-telling their tales
Now the petals are falling
From the blood roses in bloom
As I hear you calling
From inside of your room
Betrayal and trust,
Are only loyal to lust
As ashes remain numb,
To the grips of your touch
Your decency's lost,
Inside a room without doors,
As your trapped under the promise
A silhouette of something more
Rest your soul on the shards
The shards of broken glass
As you then come to terms
With images you're trying to look past
Under the weight of the world
How heavy is the cross that you bear
Is it constricting your flight
And have your broken wings begun to tear
Betrayal and trust,
Are only loyal to lust
As ashes remain numb,
To the grips of your touch
Your decency's lost,
Inside a room without doors,
As your trapped under the promise
A silhouette of something more
Now you sit and weep,
In a room without doors
'Cause there's no happy ending,
To this story of yours
What will you do,

CLYDE HURLSTON

When the lights fade to black
And your soul's once again,
Caught under attack
Betrayal and trust,
Are only loyal to lust
As ashes remain numb,
To the grips of your touch
Your decency's lost,
Inside a room without doors,
As your trapped under the promise
A silhouette of something more

SMOKE & MIRRORS

Bear witness to the coming of this age
As the ink dries on this page
Lightning strikes in the sky
Watch your notions wither and die
Listen to words long gone unspoken
As the mold lays crumbled and broken
Question the fight in the dog
Unchained, he chases you through the fog
Shame and blame!
The name of this game!
Even through the smoke and mirrors
My state of mind is becoming much clearer
Once was blind, but now I see
Digestion of you is not good for me
Tantalize my favorite parts
Vandalize my sacred heart
Take my good points make a list
And then lay me down like this
Tattoo your favorites on my chest
And pick out what you like best
Then pierce my heart until it bleeds
Pain's what the masochist needs
Shame and blame!
The name of this game!
Even through the smoke and mirrors
My state of mind is becoming much clearer
Once was blind, but now I see
Digestion of you is not good for me
If my life truly looked like this
Would you come bestow a kiss
To the one that looked like death
But had life's answers on his breath
Would you embrace or would you run
If you knew your life's outcome
Psychic visions are not healthy
For the one who sees may become wealthy
Shame and blame!

CLYDE HURLSTON

The name of this game!
Even through the smoke and mirrors
My state of mind is becoming much clearer
Once was blind, but now I see
Digestion of you is not good for me

STAR IN A TRAGEDY

The curtains begin to raise
But there's no audience
And my feelings define
What the word haunting is
But still I must perform
And imagine the sound of applause
Like a puppet on his strings
And the reason is because
They call me pessimist
Because I point out the bad
And I point out the things
That we've never had
But I'm the only one who finds
Victory inside of defeat
So my life is not broken
But it's far from complete
Now I'm dawning the mask
Of a permanent smile
On the other foot lies the shoe
And it's time to walk a mile
Inside of a world
Where it's okay to pretend
But I'm a star in a tragedy
Will my performance ever end
They call me pessimist
Because I point out the bad
And I point out the things
That we've never had
But I'm the only one who finds
Victory inside of defeat
So my life is not broken
But it's far from complete...

CLYDE HURLSTON

WHEN THE ANGELS FALL

When you said the love of the Lord
Will let you bathe in the light
Inside you struck a chord
'Cause they think the way you're livin' is right
And I see the look that's on your face
As arrogance collides with grace
Now your wings begin to ignite
You better clutch your Bible tight
Recite me lines
From your good book
'Cause the higher up you go,
The further down you look
But the righteous get judged,
Just like us all
But it's much worse,
When the angels begin to fall
Now you look at me as I laugh
At something that we both know
You forgot the most important half
Of the phrase about reaping what you sow
Nothing is hidden from His view
He knows every single thing you do
But you tried so hard to conceal
Until your outer layer began to peel
Recite me lines
From your good book
'Cause the higher up you go,
The further down you look
But the righteous get judged,
Just like us all
But it's much worse,
When the angels begin to fall
Smell the pain as your wings begin to burn
Feel regret from lessons never learned
I warned one day you'd have your turn
Now does your foolish heart still yearn
To recite me lines

BROKEN SKY

From your good book
'Cause the higher up you go,
The further down you look
But the righteous get judged,
Just like us all
But it's much worse,
When the angels begin to fall...

BITTER TONGUES

When you're living your dream
And you're working to the scene
You start forgetting to call
So they think you're starting to screen
Trying to erase all the past
While you're living so fast
And they can't deal with the fact
They keep coming in last
So now you hear the whispers
And you catch their dirty gaze
But they don't seem to notice
That you're hip to all their ways
They're far too old to act this young
But you're on the tip of bitter tongues
They hate the taste of your success
So they try to make your life a mess
They're far too old to act this young
But you're on the tip of bitter tongues
They hate the smiles before their eyes
So they try to tear you down with lies
While you're living your life
And enjoying your nights
They count every single day
That your name's been up in lights
And they think if they pray
They'll discover a way
To press control-alt-delete
And erase their pain today
So now you hear the whispers
And you catch their dirty gaze
But they don't seem to notice
That you're hip to all their ways
They're far too old to act this young
But you're on the tip of bitter tongues
They hate the taste of your success
So they try to make your life a mess
They're far too old to act this young
But you're on the tip of bitter tongues
They hate the smiles before their eyes
So they try to tear you down with lies.

SWIMMING UPSTREAM...

Embraced by the freezing cold
In its liquid form
Swimming against the tide
Is not the norm
But you're headstrong
Won't listen to warnings
Never in a million years
Did you expect what happened this morning
Your intentions were good
But the ship never would sail
So you jumped in head-first
With the fear that you'd fail
Now it's left you here
Foolishly swimming upstream
Inside the reality
Of your broken dream
There's no one to save you
From the grips of your plight
Wanted to prove them wrong
But they turned out to be right
Should I give you my hand
Because I hate to see you like this
You reject me again
And disappear inside the abyss
Your intentions were good
But the ship never would sail
So you jumped in head-first
With the fear that you'd fail
Now it's left you here
Foolishly swimming upstream
Inside the reality
Of your broken dream
My words, won't heal your pride
Offered you advice, but you brushed me aside
Now you're a failure, bitter is your aftertaste
Keep blaming me, for the life that you waste
Your intentions were good

CLYDE HURLSTON

But the ship never would sail
So you jumped in head-first
With the fear that you'd fail
Now it's left you here
Foolishly swimming upstream
Inside the reality
Of your broken dream
My words, won't heal your pride
Offered you advice, but you brushed me aside
Now you're a failure, bitter is your aftertaste
Keep blaming me, for the life that you waste...

TASTE OF DEMISE

Peel away a layer of me
Then feel free to peel away the next
'Cause first we stopped talking
And then we stopped having sex
I can't taste your kiss
On the lips that spew these lies
I refuse to live like this
Seeing that look in your eyes
Our demise is on the horizon
And it's me that you've been despising
You claim I've wronged you much
But I can't live life without feeling your touch
If you want to end this now
All you'll have to do is show me how
Your stance on this will not break or bend
I can taste our love is reaching its end
Peel away a layer of lust
Ashes to ashes, while I become dust
In your hands, so filled with might
Another night shall commence with a fight
Spout your remarks, into my blackened heart
While I'm tearing your clothing apart
Place you upon this countertop
Keep yelling at me, I don't want you to stop
I part your legs, without reason or rhyme
Baby, let me taste your love one last time
Our demise is on the horizon
And it's me that you've been despising
You claim I've wronged you much
But I can't live life without feeling your touch
If you want to end this now
All you'll have to do is show me how
Your stance on this will not break or bend
I can taste our love is reaching its end
Once kicking and screaming has reached its' end
I will still feel your nails, dig into my skin
Pleasure taste better, when it's chased down by pain

CLYDE HURLSTON

The more I hurt you, the more it pours down like rain
Our demise is on the horizon
And it's me that you've been despising
You claim I've wronged you much
But I can't live life without feeling your touch
If you want to end this now
All you'll have to do is show me how
Your stance on this will not break or bend
I can taste our love is reaching its end...

THE DARK ROOM

This place is cold and lonely
It seems like no one is welcome
Smiles grace this man's face
But the occurrence is seldom
He buries his pain in the lens
And then he always pretends
That this day will be the last
His life like a picture, his eyes won't look past
I guess it's safe to assume,
That his pain will consume
So he's wasting his life,
Locked inside of this dark room
He says he's come to find,
That this world just isn't kind
So the negatives are placed,
Back inside his frame of mind
The red light shines down
On his faults and insecurities
Craves to see the good times
But that roll of film is empty
His life a monochrome snapshot
Yet he still dreams in color
Her picture lies in the same spot
He won't move on, because he still loves her
I guess it's safe to assume,
That his pain will consume
So he's wasting his life,
Locked inside of this dark room
He says he's come to find,
That this world just isn't kind
So the negatives are placed,
Back inside his frame of mind
The camera's flash,
Truly a sight for sore eyes
Twenty-three down,
But he still has four tries
For exposure,

CLYDE HURLSTON

To her fading memory
An eight by ten in his mind,
Of what was and will never be
I guess it's safe to assume,
That his pain will consume
So he's wasting his life,
Locked inside of this dark room
He says he's come to find,
That this world just isn't kind
So the negatives are placed,
Back inside his frame of mind...

THE MASOCHIST IN ME

Now let's pretend that you're divine
Say things to tantalize my senses
But don't step too far outside that line
And don't raise up your defenses
Because I want perfection
No flaws to be seen or detected
If you want to be my selection
Or expect to get rejected
Oh yes my mistress
You don't know how much I've missed this
This punishment that I live to feel
I'll bleed dry my pleasures
As you confiscate my treasures
Close these shackles and tighten up your seal
Now let's pretend this world's serene
As you leave your marks on me
We'll re-enact your favorite scene
Oh, what a performer I can be
I'll be there to wipe your feet
As I lay here outside your door
You'll think that I'm just being sweet
Hey, that's what nice guys are for
Oh yes my mistress
You don't know how much I've missed this
This punishment that I live to feel
I'll bleed dry my pleasures
As you confiscate my treasures
Close these shackles and tighten up your seal
Oh yes, I am a masochist
There's no sense in unmasking this
Because you're blind if you can't see
This masochist living deep inside of me
The one you want is me
So come here and admonish me
If pain is what you want to inflict
Then make it last, just don't make it quick
Oh yes my mistress

CLYDE HURLSTON

You don't know how much I've missed this
This punishment that I live to feel
I'll bleed dry my pleasures
As you confiscate my treasures
Close these shackles and tighten up your seal...

THE NEW ADDICTION

These visions of a vixen
Have shown greater men than me
That we all will falter
And prove that greater men can be
Capable of falling
Once they lose their grip
But it's only when we plummet
That we can right the ship
I've been dreaming baby
The want's become a need
And you're the new addiction
That I would die to feed
My eyes inhale your grace
While the veins you're swimming through
Say you'll be my drug
And I'll overdose on you
From the top of your glowing crown
To the bottom of your weary feet
I'll caress your shining skin
And feel the beating heart beneath
And as I taste your lips
Synapses are screaming at my brain
But once I feel your fingertips
I doubt an ounce of me will complain
I've been dreaming baby
The want's become a need
And you're the new addiction
That I would die to feed
My eyes inhale your grace
While the veins you're swimming through
Say you'll be my drug
And I'll overdose on you
So you can caress me baby
Just grope each forbidden place
For I long to see that look
As it washed across your face
And it's a look that lovers see

CLYDE HURLSTON

When they find the instrument
That will take them to that special place
Where only the Gods should have went
I've been dreaming baby
The want's become a need
And you're the new addiction
That I would die to feed
My eyes inhale your grace
While the veins you're swimming through
Say you'll be my drug
And I'll overdose on you
So in closing I'll only say a little more
Before my welcome's surely worn
But you should know that you were mine
Since that fateful day you were born…

BUTTERFLY SUICIDE

She tries to fly with broken wings
Torn and frayed from spoken things
That she always took to heart
She reaches for a sky turned crystal blue
And if she leaves I'll miss her too
But she's sure to fall apart
She's a goddess to me
But she's too modest to be
The girl she keeps locked up inside
She doesn't know how much she's worth
So she wants to leave this Earth
Sounds like another case of butterfly suicide
She tries to fly amongst the clouds
Where Heaven's often found
Says from here the skies don't seem so gray
Up there she feels no pain
And can't tell when it starts to rain
But if she came down, she'd hear me say…
She's a goddess to me
But she's too modest to be
The girl she keeps locked up inside
She doesn't know how much she's worth
So she wants to leave this Earth
Sounds like another case of butterfly suicide
Darling put down the knife
And start living your life
Because there's so much more than what we're shown…
Put your trust into me
'Cause it'd be then that you'd see
That you never were alone….
Because you're a goddess to me
And you're too modest to be
The girl you keep locked up inside
Who doesn't know how much she's worth
So she wants to leave this Earth
And I am trying to prevent,
Another case of butterfly suicide

VICIOUS CIRCLE

This is the story of a girl with her mother's eyes
Who often told her father's lies
Whose little sister always cries
Everytime their brother flies
So high on methamphetamines
Part of the experimenting scene
Foolish friends they call him brave
I'll call him resident of an early grave
The vicious circle is coming 'round again
And who's child will be caught within
Fill your time with what matters least
As these children try to tame this beast
Sticks and stones break her bones
But names said they'd never hurt her
All the boys think she's oh so easy
But mommy says she's just a little flirter
What's left for a child without guidance
There's just sex or maybe violence
And it's up to them to choose
If parents don't save their kids,
Then everybody's gonna lose
The vicious circle is coming 'round again
And who's child will be caught within
Fill your time with what matters least
As these children try to tame this beast
What is going on today
What is making our children stray
Will these parents ever save their child
Or let them continue running wild
The vicious circle is coming 'round again
And who's child will be caught within
Fill your time with what matters least
As these children try to tame this beast
Save our children
Before they're gone for good
I'd save them all
If I only could

BROKEN SKY

But I'm not a hero
I'm just a normal man
And there is something
That you need to understand
The vicious circle is coming 'round again
And who's child will be caught within
Fill your time with what matters least
As these children try to tame this beast...

CLYDE HURLSTON

SAID THE FLOWER TO THE VINE

Oh, little dandelion.
My how fast you've grown.
Spent your days searching far and wide,
Look how fast the time has flown.
But, tell me... truly...
Are you happy now?
Having gone and spread yourself so thin
That your seeds blossomed discontent?
Have you felt the pains of wasted youth,
As you wondered where it went?
Forgetting that here inside the present tense,
You're a broken soul that's bare.
Confused, mistaken up for down
While here's starting to mirror there.
But if we're being honest now,
There are some things i have to know
Did you consider this a last resort?
Or just a place where you felt safe to grow?
Tell me, did you seek to gain attention,
From every passerby?
With the fear they would only see your gifts,
If you displayed them here beneath the sky.
Oh, darling, I know, I know.
You weren't wrong to hope, per se.
But still they overlooked the fact
That you were beautiful in your own way.
In this world, efforts are oft for naught
For we're specks of dust inside the wind
We're at its mercy, once we're caught.
Then we're forced to move on again.
Ever onward, tumbling through the days
Until they then give way to night
And the way you live is far from wrong
But i know that you're not feeling right
For i have felt that way myself
Still being honest, like I said
It's the reason why I'm now sharing these

Words ringing loudly in my head
But it was as I was saying this
That her face began to change
And flashed a look with angry eyes
Then started acting strange
'Cause I guess she felt interrogated
Or even cross-examined in a court
So it was then she wished to shut me up
By offering this loud retort,
"For starters, I'm not just any flower.
Hell, you're looking at a rose.
A better form was never seen,
So it's often that I'm chose
But you call yourself some kind of vine,
But in truth, you're closer to a tree.
With roots dug in as deep as yours,
You don't know how good where else could be.
While sitting here, and growing old
Is all that you can do
Unaware that you are a giant fool
And the world's biggest sap is you
So save your condescending wisdom
And advice you've offered up
Because i think that you will be alone
Until the day your coffin's shut
And you can sit here and play the sage
As if all the answers are possessed
By that thing inside your head
And the foolish thing within your chest.
'Cause I'm too busy living life
To be concerned with what you think
And i could be somebody's wife
By the next time that you blink
So focus on your business
And i will concentrate on mine"
Yes, these were all the things
A gorgeous flower had once said to a vine.

CLYDE HURLSTON

THE MATHEMATICS OF SUICIDE

You say that life
Is no longer worth living
An early departure
Is the gift that you're giving
To yourself
You can't take this anymore
That is not the answer
Won't you please unlock this door
There's the cut, the cut
From the blade, the blade
And the wound you made
You won't pause or stop
And your door is locked
Oh God, I curse this day
There's the blood, the blood
It makes a stain, a stain
You're caving into your pain
You're having a breakdown
And not a breakthrough
Tell me how to save you
Deliver a swift kick
Remove the door from its hinges
Rush to pull you back
From what you call the fringes
You say your life
Isn't full of glamor
Your wrist is a nail
And this knife is your hammer
There's the cut, the cut
From the blade, the blade
And the wound you made
You won't pause or stop
And your door is locked
Oh God, I curse this day
There's the blood, the blood
It makes a stain, a stain
You're caving into your pain

BROKEN SKY

You're having a breakdown
And not a breakthrough
Tell me how to save you
Add a knife to your wrist
And make a motion like this
And you're taking away from your bliss
Your heart and soul will divide
And the hurt's only multiplied
These are the mathematics of suicide
There's the cut, the cut
From the blade, the blade
And the wound you made
You won't pause or stop
And your door is locked
Oh God, I curse this day
There's the blood, the blood
It makes a stain, a stain
You're caving into your pain
You're having a breakdown
And not a breakthrough
Tell me how to save you
And please put down your knife...

MORNING STAR

In this abyss I lay
Enshrouded in a welcome black
Hoping you'll come out to play
And provide me with the light I lack
For I long to be
Embraced by divinity
Cause I seek to be redeemed
By the goddess in my lasting dream
Who's shining like the morning star
I know exactly where you are
Glowing brightly in my nightly view
I would gladly burn for touching you
But the burn I'd feel on fingertips
Would not compare to aching lips
That got to taste the sweetest love
To ever lay beneath the skies above
Eve was product of a rib
While Lilith was made from Earth
Submission fit the former well
But the latter realized her worth
And decided that she would never bow
She would only stand beside
But after centuries have passed
The goddess that I wish to be inside
Is shining like the morning star
And I know exactly where you are
Glowing brightly in my nightly view
I would gladly burn for touching you
But the burn I'd feel on fingertips
Would not compare to aching lips
That got to taste the sweetest love
To ever lay beneath the skies above
And still I'm lying motionless
Hoping my dreams will bring me peace
But the fires that they ignite
Seem like their burning will never cease
Until their smoke begins to choke the sky

BROKEN SKY

As a signal to my morning star
Informing her that she's forever mine
Even if her orbit longs to take her far
She'll still be shining like the morning star
I know exactly where you are
Glowing brightly in my nightly view
I would gladly burn for touching you
But the burn I'd feel on fingertips
Would not compare to aching lips
That got to taste the sweetest love
To ever lay beneath the skies above
But I would walk the Earth to prove
That I'm content in stumbling
Toward you as you start to move
In ways that are surely humbling
Such as choosing me to be the one
To witness your return to mortal form
And when the night is said and done
I will do far more than keep you warm...

CLYDE HURLSTON

THAT'S JUST LIFE

There's a mouse just outside the window
A hawk peers down from high inside a tree
It makes me sit and wonder,
If the mouse will make it under
As talons pierce his fur,
He calls out to me:
That's just life...
Don't spend your waking moments,
Consumed with tomorrow
Passing by delight,
While entrenched in your sorrow
Just try to find a way,
To live only for today
Because it's more important,
Than any yesterday
A hunter's bullet hits the hawk now
All the mouse can do is fall down
He races for the garden,
Without begging any pardons
He turns toward me slow,
And says see I told you so
That's just life...
Don't spend your waking moments,
Consumed with tomorrow
Passing by delight,
While entrenched in your sorrow
Just try to find a way,
To live only for today
Because it's more important,
Than any yesterday
The mouse feels relief from danger
But in the distance there's a stranger
Nowhere to hide so he decides to run
A cat gives chase just for a little fun
The mouse will never see another night
The cat pounces down and takes a bite
But just before he takes a gulp and swallow

BROKEN SKY

He says here is some advice that you should follow
Don't spend your waking moments,
Consumed with tomorrow
Passing by delight,
While entrenched in your sorrow
Just try to find a way,
To live only for today
Because it's more important,
Than any yesterday...

CLYDE HURLSTON

END OF ACT 2

"A cloud does not know why it moves in just such a direction and at such a speed... It feels an impulsion... This is the place to go now. But the sky knows the reasons and the patterns behind all clouds, and you will know, too, when you lift yourself high enough to see beyond horizons."

-Richard Bach

"In the sky there are always answers and explanations for everything: every pain, every suffering, joy and confusion."

-Ishmael Beah

CLYDE HURLSTON

3
A COMPROMISE IN NATURE

"In nature, nothing is perfect and everything is perfect. Trees can be contorted, bent in weird ways, and they are still beautiful."

-Alice Walker

"DARKNESS TAKES THE DOVE"
ART BY VALISA BERNARDINO

CLYDE HURLSTON

THE PUSH AND THE SHOVE

It's time I stepped outside of myself
And took a look around
At how your life revolves and evolves
But you never seem to make a sound
Is it that I'm deaf to your all thoughts
Or that have I heard this all before
It's like the piercing words you say
Are equal to the slamming of a door
This is not about a love,
It's just about a push,
That's followed by a shove
I try to push the issue,
Back into its place
And you just shove it,
Right back into my face
This roller-coaster ride,
Has left us taped and tied
Neither wants to reveal,
What's hidden deep inside
We just keep pretending,
There's an issue that we're defending
But the truth of it all,
Is our fences still need mending
These words came to me in dreams
And these nightmare interpretations
Describing the bliss we once felt
That shifted towards this devastation
One nation, crumbles under weight
Pointing fingers at the ones who wait
For the other to finally accept the blame
And bear the brunt of the other's flame
The scales are shifting because of weight
Tip in your favor, because of hate
But when we're good,
It feels like destiny
But there's days like today,
When you keep testing me

BROKEN SKY

This roller-coaster ride,
Has left us taped and tied
Neither wants to reveal,
What's hidden deep inside
We just keep pretending,
There's an issue that we're defending
But the truth of it all,
Is our fences still need mending
I'm tired of the hiding,
And I'm tired of the fighting
When emotions keep sliding,
It's hard to do the right thing
But what if we promised that we'd try
And neither of us lied
Would that finally reveal
What's hidden deep inside
What's hidden deep inside of me
The things you've tried to see
Maybe I'll let you see inside of me today
If you did the same... someday
Because this roller-coaster ride,
Has left us taped and tied
Neither wants to reveal,
What's hidden deep inside
We just keep pretending,
There's an issue that we're defending
But the truth of it all,
Is that our fences still need mending...

CLYDE HURLSTON

THE SCALES OF JUSTICE

Will your actions inspire
Or were they hollow
Have you blazed a trail
That we can blindly follow
You get a rush from things
That do you harm
Find you on 8th & Ocean
With holes in your arm
Extra extra!
Who will I read about
Complain about the attention
You can't do without
What will you do
When the lights begin to fade
Will the good deeds
Outweigh the mistakes you've made
They put your pictures
On their walls
Get you high enough
Just to watch you fall
Driven around in nice cars
By your hired help
Tell me of the pain
And suffering that you've felt
But you spend your money
On those designer clothes
And I find you on Capitol Hill
With powder on your nose
Extra extra!
Who will I read about
Complain about the attention
You can't do without
What will you do
When the lights begin to fade
Will the good deeds
Outweigh the mistakes you've made
They cover your scandals

BROKEN SKY

In their magazines
Yet the music I make
Is what you wanna call obscene
Here it comes, hot off the presses
On the front page, should lie this message
Don't fuck with me, if you want to live
I just want the attention of your kids
What will you do
When the lights begin to fade
Will the good deeds
Outweigh the mistakes you've made
They put your pictures
On their walls
Get you high enough
Just to watch you fall
What will you do
When the lights begin to fade
Will the good deeds
Outweigh the mistakes you've made
They cover your scandals
In their magazines
Yet it's the art I wanna make
That you will call obscene...

CLYDE HURLSTON

SIRENS ARE FLASHING

They say this world
Can be a lonely place for you
Everything goes right
For only a selected few
But that's okay
You can always turn to me
Because you've got a point of view
That I can learn to see
You sent me signals,
And I'm not receiving them
I sent you messages,
And you're not believing them
The sirens are flashing now,
Have you gone blind to them
Maybe God is telling you,
To find your way back to him
You say this world
Is so very far from serene
So they like to claim
You paint such a depressing scene
Under such scrutiny
We're always under attack
Life isn't always gray
Just because I dress in jet black
You sent me signals,
And I'm not receiving them
I sent you messages,
And you're not believing them
The sirens are flashing now,
Have you gone blind to them
Maybe God is telling you,
To find your way back to him
The sight of flashing lights
Is piercing the sky, of these star-filled nights
A siren's scream, the soul's alarm
It shall awaken the ones, aiming to do you harm
You sent me signals,

BROKEN SKY

And I'm not receiving them
I sent you messages,
And you're not believing them
The sirens are flashing now,
Have you gone blind to them
Maybe God is telling you,
To find your way back to him...

CLYDE HURLSTON

THE SWEET SOUNDS OF REVENGE

I put my dreams on hold
To help you with reaching your own
By the time I had opened my eyes
I discovered that you had left me alone
I acknowledged your goals
Admonished each consequence
Solitude left in your wake
What can be said in your defense
Betrayal is the stake,
That's piercing my heart
As what we were,
Started falling apart
You just turned away,
And relinquished your hold
These are the sweet sounds of revenge,
Escaping from a heart that has frozen cold
Did you think you'd remain
On the perch I once placed you upon
If so, your thought was in vain
Your allure has faded and gone
Now your dreams have fallen flat
In my good graces you wish to return
But as I look back
You were a lesson, that I needed to learn
Because betrayal is the stake,
That's piercing my heart
As what we were,
Started falling apart
You just turned away,
And relinquished your hold
These are the sweet sounds of revenge,
Escaping from a heart that has frozen cold....
I've been trying to repair,
The soul that you've broken
Entrenched in despair,
Over words unspoken
Now you've been humbled,

BROKEN SKY

After you left me for dead
And as I look down on your nothing,
I'll just thank you instead
For using the stake,
That's piercing my heart
As what we were,
Started falling apart
You just turned away,
And relinquished your hold
These are the sweet sounds of revenge,
Escaping from a heart that has frozen cold....

CLYDE HURLSTON

UNDER THE INFLUENCE OF ART

With drifting thoughts of yesterday
He thought he could escape
So he stuffed that powder in his nose
And then he put on his cape
Said that he would rid the world
Of suffering and crime
The orderlies looked at him
And said this man's out his mind
And now this troubled man
Thinks that he can fly
Jumps on the window sill,
He's headed to the sky
Is there no one here,
Who can stop this man tonight?
If they want to bring him down,
They had best start with kryptonite
So now he grabs a rusty knife
And carves an 'S' into his chest
Said he waited his entire life
But this calling wouldn't rest
He displays all his wounds
And wears his symbol proud
Someone asked him who he is
And so he'd repeat it loud
And now this troubled man
Thinks that he can fly
Jumps on the window sill,
He's headed to the sky
Is there no one here,
Who can stop this man tonight?
If they want to bring him down,
They had best start with kryptonite
He feels like a hero inside his heart
But some say he's under the influence of art
They blame everything,
Except they drugs he's on
But let's see how he acts,

BROKEN SKY

When the drugs are gone
And now this troubled man
Thinks that he can fly
Jumps on the window sill,
He's headed to the sky
Is there no one here,
Who can stop this man tonight?
If they want to bring him down,
They had best start with kryptonite
Yes, this troubled man
Once thought that he could fly
Now he sits and wonders why
No one tried to save him from himself
If art was so bad for his health

UNMASK

Life is your grandest stage
Performing feats for the weak
Can I find it a bit strange
They hang on every word you never speak
A symphony of defeat
Moving in silence across the screen
Like a phantom without an opera
You're best when you go unseen
Throughout our history
We've loved the mystery
But it's time you unmask
Or is that too great a task
Wrapped up in shadows
Embracing the darkness
And where this man goes
Just proves that he's heartless
He plays his instrument of death
Often shaped like a knife
His performance steals the breath
And his encore takes the life
Throughout our history
We've loved the mystery
But it's time you unmask
Or is that too great a task
Sure, there is no witness
To this story I'll tell
Just a protagonist
That brings you greetings From Hell
That's why throughout our history
We've loved the mystery
But it's time you unmask
Or is that too great a task?

WAR FOR A SOUL

The devil has my feet,
While God is grasping my hands
In the distance there's an hourglass,
That's no longer catching the sands
Each wants a chance,
To fill this hole in my heart
But this war for my soul,
Has been tearing me apart
I'd go to hell and face the devil
To remove his control
I'd go to hell and face the devil
To loosen his grip on my soul
I scream for Satan to fight me
And may Jesus help smite thee
As I reach for what I've buried within
And I hope to somehow find it again
A wise man said the ashes of your past,
Are what you cannot look past
Young man you're dying within
So tell me what is ailing you my friend
I quickly responded
With an expression desponded
And said in case you didn't hear me
I'll say this again
I'd go to hell and face the devil
To remove his control
I'd go to hell and face the devil
To loosen his grip on my soul
I scream for Satan to fight me
And may Jesus help smite thee
As I reach for what I've buried within
And I hope to somehow find it again
A demon approached me
And threatened to choke me
And I almost welcomed him
But then I got into my right mind
And said not in this lifetime

CLYDE HURLSTON

The outlook for my betrayal is grim
I'd go to hell and face the devil
To remove his control
I'd go to hell and face the devil
To loosen his grip on my soul
I scream for Satan to fight me
And may Jesus help smite thee
As I reach for what I've buried within
And now more than ever,
I hope to somehow find it again...

WASTED LIFE

Come on in, and have a seat
Tell me a story of your wasted life
Here's a pen, write it neat
Just to make sure you're tellin' it right
Tell me have you fallen prey
To such stark perceptions
Or were you forced to use
Both your heart and soul as weapons
It was then his eyes were locked and loaded
Until his thoughts exploded
Overwhelmed by what he suppressed
A wasted life is never truly at rest
Come on in, and have a seat
Tell me a story of your wasted life
Here's a page, from my own
Just to show you that you're not alone
I too have fallen prey
To a world that won't look my way
I've let true feelings go unspoken
Now my heart and soul lie battered and broken
It was then his eyes were locked and loaded
Until his thoughts exploded
Overwhelmed by what he suppressed
A wasted life is never truly at rest
I truly believe it's okay to fight
If your enemy's become just a little bit clearer
And if you fight, you better be able to live
With the person that you see in the mirror
It was then his eyes were locked and loaded
Until his thoughts exploded
Overwhelmed by what he suppressed
A wasted life is never truly at rest.

CLYDE HURLSTON

THE RETURN

A gentle rustling in the trees
And the gentle roaring of the seas
Could bring me back to you
Yes, it could bring me back to you
A subtle movement of the skies
Gone with the blinking of your eyes
Could bring you back to me
Yes, it could bring you back to me
The gentle tapping of the rain
And the smile when you hear it tap again
Could bring me back to you
Yes, it could bring me back to you
The joy of children hard at play
Brings laughter 'round your way
And could bring you back to me
Yes, it could bring you back to me
A dog barking in the night
At a volume so I can hear it right
Will bring me back to you
Yes, it will bring me back to you
A cat hides beneath a car
In fear of the tyrants that we are
Could bring you back to me
Yes, it will bring you back to me
Three birds perched on top a branch
Sing their song as if by chance
The sound will bring me back to you
Yes, it will bring me back to you
The scent of candles still in burn
Tells me I can handle your return
So it will bring you back to me
Yes, it will bring you back to me
And if this is the last few lines I should write
Remember that I will be all yours tonight
Because these words brought you back to me
After all, where else should you be?

WHEN THE MOON RUNS RED

How much will I lose
Before I start to gain
It's this lack of pleasure
That has caused me pain
But no one can see through
This layer of invisible skin
Unaware of the treasure
That I harbor within
When the moon runs red
These thoughts float through my head
When the moon runs red
I reminisce over things unsaid
Then I look into her eyes
I see redemption's at hand
I thought they were only lies
But it seems that God's got a plan
And maybe she was a gift
That was given to me
'Cause she can make tomorrow
Worth livin' to see
When the moon runs red
These thoughts float through my head
When the moon runs red
I reminisce over things unsaid
She said nevermind that now
Because I am here with you
So I'll forget the world
And what it has put me through
I didn't realize how numb
That I had truly become
Until she walked into my life
Quickly erased any feeling of strife
I can't put into words
My entire feelings for her
But I would die to keep her from harm
And then be reborn inside of her arms
When the moon runs red

CLYDE HURLSTON

These thoughts float through my head
When the moon runs red
I reminisce over things unsaid
She said nevermind that now
Because I am here with you
So I'll forget the world
And what it has put me through.

WHERE LOVE ONCE LIVED

The hatred flows just like a stream
Inside the things you say but never mean
Sanity seems just outside your range
I'm foolish to think you will ever change
Pick a spot to insert your knife
Cut your way back into my life
As the blade makes love to skin
I'll stitch the heart you pierced within
As you walked into the room,
you slid the lid from off the tomb
My soul is dry and withered,
You've been known to make it bloom
The inscription on the lid,
The result of things you did
It says pleasure now resides,
In the place where love once lived
Pleasantries are cloaked with spite
Inside the things we both do at night
How I feel when I'm inside of you
As your heart and soul divide in two
Bitter tongues inside of playful lips
Judgment rains off your fingertips
It seems as if you won't approve
The things I do when you're in the mood
As you walked into the room,
you slid the lid from off the tomb
My soul is dry and withered,
You've been known to make it bloom
The inscription on the lid,
The result of things you did
It says pleasure now resides,
In the place where love once lived
The noise of the door's loudest creak
Penetrates like the words you speak
Like when you denounced my love
Acting as if you were high above
The reach of this mortal man

CLYDE HURLSTON

Who does what he can
To keep you satisfied
But what you don't know
Today's the day he died
Today he died...
Girl bring me back to life... please...
As you walked into the room,
You slid the lid from off the tomb
My soul is dry and withered,
You've been known to make it bloom
The inscription on the lid,
The result of things you did
It says pleasure now resides,
In the place where love once lived.

YOUR DISEASE

You know you're pretentious
That's what I've come to find
And yet my best intentions
Are what you had in mind
What if I don't believe you
And I decided to call your bluff
Would you settle for what you took
Would that ever be enough
Justice keeps escaping us
Because your actions are raping us
Have the world beneath your thumb
But I will not succumb
I'd rather die on my feet
Than to live on my knees
Begging to you
To spare me from your disease
This is not a song is what you say
Claim that I've exaggerated much
That your rule won't end today
You're invincible to touch
Am I taking things to heart
Should I let go of this little hurt
Or should I keep biting my tongue
Until blood soaks my fucking shirt
Justice keeps escaping us
Because your actions are raping us
Have the world beneath your thumb
But I will not succumb
I'd rather die on my feet
Than to live on my knees
Begging to you
To spare me from your disease
You're nothing to me
You're lower than scum
I hate what you are
I hate what you've become
I hate the sight of your face

CLYDE HURLSTON

I wish I could erase
Your existence on Earth
So in hell you could take your place
Justice keeps escaping us
Because your actions are raping us
Have the world beneath your thumb
But I will not succumb
I'd rather die on my feet
Than to live on my knees
Begging to you
To spare me from your disease.

THE PHOENIX

As they walk together she takes a peek
A wayward glance, at one who doesn't speak
He just walks slow, like a passing wind
Like a fleeting breath on impatient skin
She looks at him, with x-ray eyes
And sees he's not like those other guys
Then things start to get a little strange
She looks again, and he starts to change
Who knows what's going through her head?
Now that his eyes are flashing red
Six words are what he says to her
And then he spreads his wings
While embracing the pain it brings
The phoenix has begun to stir...
In a flash, his wings went away
And she is left without words to say
He acts like nothing has occurred
Like it's everyday the creature stirred
But my dear that isn't true
These events are inspired by the sight of you
And by the way he used to be
Which will cause, what you're about to see
Who knows what's going through her head?
Now that his eyes are flashing red
Six words are what he says to her
And then he spreads his wings
While embracing the pain it brings
The phoenix has begun to stir...
While she's seduced, by the lovely flashes
The man she loves, now stands in the ashes
Of the life, he once chose to lead
And with a whisper, the world took heed...
I am reborn...
Who knows what's going through her head?
Now that his eyes are flashing red
Six words are what he says to her
And then he spreads his wings

While embracing the pain it brings
The phoenix has begun to stir...
While she's seduced, by the lovely flashes
The man she loves, now stands in the ashes
Of the life, he once chose to lead
And with a whisper, the world took heed...
I am reborn...
While she's seduced, by the lovely flashes
The man she loves, now stands in the ashes
Of the life, he once chose to lead
And with one scream, the world took heed...
I AM REBORN!!!

SPITEFUL SERENADE

If pleasure was a stone
Aimed at your fragile soul
I would hope it breaks
The next time I'm in control
You justify your lies
Behind shards of colored glass
While resting on the pews
Dreaming about lovers past
Lay down and open wide
So that I can provide
A new thorn for your side
As you confuse your pain with pride
If God only knew
How much I hated you
Would He think
That love is overrated too
So as you lie
In this bed that you've made
Open your ears
To this spiteful serenade
You lift your legs
Toward the tinted skies
Exposed your love
To many different guys
But you're rejecting me
Because I'm not like them
And then ask me why
My outlook is so grim
Lay down and open wide
So that I can provide
A new thorn for your side
As you confuse your pain with pride
If God only knew
How much I hated you
Would He think
That love is overrated too
So as you lie

CLYDE HURLSTON

In this bed that you've made
Open your ears
To this spiteful serenade
I hate everything
But the way you taste
So I close my eyes
When I kiss your face...
How many times, have you opened wide?
And let the unworthy ones provide
The new thorn, for your unhealed side
As you see, the good in me has died!
If God only knew
How much I hated you
Would He think
That love is overrated too
So as you lie
In this bed that you've made
Open your ears
To this spiteful serenade.

UPSIDE OF DISTANCE

Romantic visions
Infect each thought
Placed with precision
And the love she brought
It's so hard to see
Her true motives
So how else should I feel
When I'm already hopeless
Forgive me for running
From what we're becoming
I'm sorry sweet darling
But I fear there'll be further scarring
It's in an instance
I see the need for distance
But in case you missed it
I'll cherish your existence
The names you were called
You're wearing them proud
Now I must rebuild my walls
'Cause you keep tearing them down
Baby I need them
To keep you at bay
And to repel the deceiving
But maybe I'll seek you today
It's in an instance
I see the need for distance
But in case you missed it
I'll cherish your existence
Love breeds passion
When fury's no longer in fashion
So it's without a hint of shame
That my heart beats to the rhythm of your name...
It's in an instance
I see the need for distance
But in case you missed it
I'll cherish your existence
Forgive me for running
From what we're becoming
I'm sorry sweet darling
But I fear there'll be further scarring...

WISHFUL TEARS

There's something I've thought about
For the past few years
If I could be a part of you
I would choose to be your tears
Now girl don't get me wrong
I don't want to see you cry
But you since you look confused
I'll tell you the reason why
I'd be conceived in your heart
And then born in your eyes
I'd softly caress your face
And watch as the time flies
And I would never forget
My feeling like this
As I died on your lips
To be reborn with a kiss
Girl I dreamt of you so much
I see you when my eyes aren't open
And I've said I love you so much
You hear it when it goes unspoken
I don't consider myself weak
But I'm helpless when I feel your touch
As a tear glides down your cheek
Listen to the words I speak
I'd be conceived in your heart
And then born in your eyes
I'd softly caress your face
And watch as the time flies
And I would never forget
My feeling like this
As I died on your lips
To be reborn with a kiss
Girl I love to see you smile
And to feel the warmth you have inside
But to see those tears you cry
It sends my soul for a ride
And the destination is unknown

But I hope my love is what I've shown
To you on this blissful day
But once again I have to say
I'd be conceived in your heart
And then born in your eyes
I'd softly caress your face
And watch as the time flies
And I would never forget
My feeling like this
As I died on your lips
To be reborn with a kiss...

UNEVEN SCALES

How do you release your breath
When it's been held for so long
And how are you affected by death
When your way of thinking is wrong
How can you consider giving
To the ones you've so often denied
And how can you measure living
When I can't tell if you're even alive
Your nature is callous
And it's shifting the balance
Of the so-called truth in your tales
For years we laid oblivious
To the fact that you're giving us
Your opinion based on these uneven scales
How we can be we angels
When we weren't blessed with our wings
And how can we be in tune with God
When we can't hear what he sings
And His voice is booming to us
Just look as it's moving the dust
That has fallen from the hourglass
I guess our time has finally passed
Your nature is callous
And it's shifting the balance
Of the so-called truth in your tales
For years we laid oblivious
To the fact that you're giving us
Your opinion based on these uneven scales
Is your glass half-full
Or half-empty
I'll give you my guess
If you continue to tempt me
With another sip of your poisonous tales
But it's a must
That I stop and think
And realize
That I don't want to drink

BROKEN SKY

I just want to balance these fucking scales...
Your nature is callous
And it's shifting the balance
Of the so-called truth in your tales
For years we laid oblivious
To the fact that you're giving us
Your opinion based on these uneven scales.

TANGLED WEBS

It seems we were destined to become
Tangled up in the webs that we've spun
Still we try to spin them again
Just to trap the ones we'll never let in
Through both time and space
She boldly walks alone
The wind blows across her face
She moves in a rhythm all her own
As if she's marching to a beat
While puddles form on the ground
The street breathes beneath her feet
In her despair she starts to drown
It seems we were destined to become
Tangled up in the webs that we've spun
Still we try to spin them again
Just to trap the ones we'll never let in
The hands release their death grip
On the seconds passing by
To witness this is a head trip
'Cause I see that look in her eye
As she approaches a random man
Who'll come to wish she never met him
But he won't understand
Until his veins run hot with her venom
It seems we were destined to become
Tangled up in the webs that we've spun
Still we try to spin them again
Just to trap the ones we'll never let in
Don't you dare,
Ask her why
Just embrace your goodbye,
Won't you little fly
Listen to the song,
The widow chose to sing
'Cause in a moment,
You won't feel a thing...
It seems we were destined to become
Tangled up in the webs that we've spun
Still we try to spin them again
Just to trap the ones we'll never let in.

ARMAGEDDON

Bullets tear through the bluest skies
As politicians tell the truest lies
Convincing us to sell our souls
In the names of securing liquid gold
That is black to sight and fuels the cars
While raping lands considered ours
All the ice has begun to melt
Mother Earth demands her pain be felt
Bear witness to horrors on the screen
As the warning signs have gone unseen
How are the children going to survive
As we broadcast armageddon live
Money's in the war not in the peace
So the fighting will never cease
The children are not safe in schools
We blame musicians when we're the fools
And the t.v. sets have raised the child
Blame actors because they're running wild
Pointing fingers has become a sport
With our leaders standing center court
Bear witness to horrors on the screen
As the warning signs have gone unseen
How are the children going to survive
As we broadcast armageddon live
Are we close to Holocaust
What will we do, when all is lost
Will the Gods hear our call
Who's to blame, when kingdoms fall
Bear witness to horrors on the screen
As the warning signs have gone unseen
How are the children going to survive
As we broadcast armageddon live.

CLYDE HURLSTON

AS CURTAINS CRASH

Like I was just a child
I would run to you
But when you're embraced by millions
What is one to you
Silence is now my favorite sound
Because it means you're not around
The only time your feet touch the ground
Is when those curtains come crashing down
With tidal waves of people
Rising before your eyes
Do you ever stop to wonder
How I digest all your lies
It's getting harder by the day
To dawn this smile of mine
When our children barely play
'Cause they're keeping track of time
Silence is now my favorite sound
Because it means you're not around
The only time your feet touch the ground
Is when those curtains come crashing down
We are nothing more than pictures
That are torn and frayed
Burning in remembrance
Of every game you played
The flames are reaching higher
To match my inner rage
So sing as much as you desire
Since your home is now a stage
Silence is now my favorite sound
Because it means you're not around
The only time your feet touch the ground
Is when those curtains come crashing down.

BLACKENED BY CLICHES

It's true that my hair's been dyed
To match this heart of mine
Blackened by cliches I've heard
That echo inside my mind
You will find someone someday
Oh these words the hollow truth
Depression is a savage beast
That has come to swallow youth
If you take my smile away
And leave it chained to my disgust
Tell them this cage you've kept me in
Has since begun to rust
And if I decide to fall today
Don't blame it on my ways
And if they ask, then I will say
My heart was blackened by cliches
It's true that my hair's been dyed
To match those eyes of yours
The ones that shine and reflect
The closing of these doors
To a place I once called a home
That has since become a cell
And you should always be alone
When you're on your way to hell
If you take my smile away
And leave it chained to my disgust
Tell them this cage you've kept me in
Has since begun to rust
And if I decide to fall today
Don't blame it on my ways
And if they ask, then I will say
My heart was blackened by cliches
Justify your every wrong
And the way you've treated me
And we we've known along
You have defeated me...
But I will rise again one day

CLYDE HURLSTON

Like a phoenix in the tales
And here is my own cliche
Over sinners the saint still prevails...
If you take my smile away
And leave it chained to my disgust
Tell them this cage you've kept me in
Has since begun to rust
And if I decide to fall today
Don't blame it on my ways
And if they ask, then I will say
My heart was blackened by cliches...

STANDING STILL

Girl your life has grinded to a halt
While screeching to a stop
But it's surely not my fault
So take your finger off the top
Of the button to self-destruct
The progress that we've made
Oh my precious little kitten
Stop acting like you're spayed
It seems he should've been your last
Because he's the one you cannot look past
And he's left you here standing still
And now to slow down's what you ask
Because I'm moving just a little bit fast
That's 'cause you keep standing still...
You say that I'm a bigger man
In more ways than one
So tell me what makes you think
That I'll do what he's done
And I don't look the way
He so often does
So tell me why you think
That I'll ever be the way he was
It seems he should've been your last
Because he's the one you cannot look past
And he's left you here standing still
And now to slow down's what you ask
Because I'm moving just a little bit fast
That's 'cause you keep standing still...
Please don't paint me condescending
But it's time you stopped pretending
That you can't live without him
When he can't live without you
That's the reason he comes crawling back
Saying your love's what he lacks
But you were never on his mind
Until you became mine...
It seems he should've been your last

CLYDE HURLSTON

Because he's the one you cannot look past
And he's left you here standing still
And now to slow down's what you ask
Because I'm moving just a little bit fast
But darling, that's only because
You keep standing still...

CHOOSE TO RISE

The place you've come to lay
Is where I used to reside
Wasting every single day
In the darkness where I'd hide
But then I crawled out
And faced the light...
He's watching now, from above us all
Counting all the times we fall
And everytime, He shuts His eyes
He's hoping that...
That we'll choose to rise
You don't have to keep
Going this way you've known
'Cause only the commandments were
Ever set in stone
So now your life
Is in your hands...
He's watching now, from above us all
Counting all the times we fall
And everytime, He shuts His eyes
He's hoping that we'll choose to rise
He's watching now, from above us all
Counting all the times we fall
And everytime, He shuts His eyes
He's hoping that...
That we'll choose to rise
The path you've chose to blaze
Was paved with your wretched ways
So continue on the path you know
And start to reap what you chose to sow..
He's watching now, from above us all
Counting all the times we fall
And everytime, He shuts His eyes
He's hoping that we'll choose to rise
He's watching now, from above us all
Counting all the times we fall
And everytime, He shuts His eyes
He's hoping that...
That we'll choose to rise.

CROSS THE LINE

She walked into her home,
Detected just the faintest smell
Of a scent she doesn't wear
From as far as she can tell
She walks on throughout
Searching for the source of said perfume
And she wasn't ready for the find
In her very own bedroom
She knew that something was amiss
'Cause she didn't get her morning kiss
And now it's ruined all her bliss
Left her job and returned to this...
Now her worst day is occuring live
As the good times start to take a dive
Dropping down to record lows
Over the secrets that she knows
She feels like pulling out her hair
'Cause evidence is scattered everywhere
And now she's played the fool
After he broke her only rule
Don't cross that line...
She sees the sheets across the floor
And underwear on top the lamp
Opens up the bathroom door
And the mirror's still slightly damp
She walks in the living room
Still ingesting all his lies
And he's unaware of his impending doom
While she's wiping tears from her eyes
She knew that something was amiss
'Cause she didn't get her morning kiss
And now it's ruined all her bliss
Left her job and returned to this...
Now her worst day is occuring live
As the good times start to take a dive
Dropping down to record lows
Over the secrets that she knows

BROKEN SKY

She feels like pulling out her hair
'Cause evidence is scattered everywhere
And now she's played the fool
After he broke her only rule
Don't cross that line...
She knew that something was amiss
'Cause she didn't get her morning kiss
And now it's ruined all her bliss
Left her job and returned to this...
She grabs a knife from the kitchen drawer
Says this won't happen to me anymore
He walks in and sees the knife
And now he's running for his life...
Now her worst day is occuring live
As the good times start to take a dive
Dropping down to record lows
Over the secrets that she knows
She feels like pulling out her hair
'Cause evidence is scattered everywhere
And now she's played the fool
After he broke her only rule
Don't cross that line...
Don't cross that line...
Don't cross that line...
Ooh, you crossed that line...
BETTER GET GONE!

CLYDE HURLSTON

DESTROY AND REBUILD

Within the confines of a mind
Have I laid broken
Breathing to pass the time
Missing the words once spoken
Tell me what I've become
Held inside this closed shell
Reaching out toward your Heaven
It seems I've chosen hell
I've tried and tried
To climb out of this hole
But down I slide
Back into the cold
With the tears that I've spilled
I must destroy and rebuild
Until my grave is filled
I will destroy and rebuild
But I don't need your sorrow
As I destroy and rebuild
For I'll be reborn tomorrow
Destroyed and rebuilt
Then you gazed into the abyss
The sights sent you reeling
Still you greet me with a kiss
Because your touch is healing
Tomorrow's wish is my command
If I do so live to see it dear
Give me your hand
And I'll survive it if you're here
I've tried and tried
To climb out of the cold
You stopped the slide
And somehow made me whole
With the tears that I've spilled
I must destroy and rebuild
Until my grave is filled
I will destroy and rebuild
But I don't need your sorrow

BROKEN SKY

As I destroy and rebuild
For I'll be reborn tomorrow
Destroyed and rebuilt
Will you help me tear down
The man I used to be
This cross that I bear now
The sight I used to see
Blind me from this world
All I wish to see is you
Hear me won't you girl
For your love is what pulls me through
With the tears that I've spilled
I must destroy and rebuild
Until my grave is filled
I will destroy and rebuild
But I don't need your sorrow
As I destroy and rebuild
For I'll be reborn tomorrow
Destroyed and rebuilt.

DIG

I sat down on a park bench
Watching birds dance on power lines
The morning has a familiar stench
I look down and see the hour's nine
The hands of time slowly spin
As I decide to take a gaze within
And it was then that a passerby
Said son, let me tell you what's on my mind
So many look towards the sky
When they can't find the reason why...
Dig deep into the words you say
To find why things don't go your way
'Cause a puzzle without hint or clues
Leaves one inside another's shoes
I sat awestruck for a moment's pass
Then regained myself just as fast
This mystery man stood hand in hand
With a woman who was in demand
By the audience she quickly drew
Said, this is why I can't be with you
So she turned and stormed away
And as she walked I heard her say
So many look towards the sky
When they can't find the reason why...
Dig deep into the words you say
To find why things don't go your way
'Cause a puzzle without hint or clues
Leaves one inside another's shoes
The moral of the story is
Treat everyday like they were gifts
And instead of looking up to the sky
Look deep inside to find...
The reasons why!
Dig deep into the words you say
To find why things don't go your way
'Cause a puzzle without hint or clues
Leaves one inside another's shoes...

DIG INTO MY HEART

Won't you dig into my heart
With your self-righteous shovel
Won't you tear me apart
Before I finally crumble
At least this way
I can say that I tried
And on this day
You'll witness the good in me die
Dig into my heart
And tell me what I've got left
'Cause living is this way
Isn't good for my health
Why can't I be happy
As I wallow in the mundane
Why am I left bitter
And defined by my shame
Won't you dig into my heart
And find something of value
Instead of the lies
That so many will sell you
I hear you say
Darling, it won't stay this way
But when I turn around
You're not to be found
Dig into my heart
And tell me what I've got left
'Cause living is this way
Isn't good for my health
Why can't I be happy
As I wallow in the mundane
Why am I left bitter
And defined by my shame
If you really chose to dig
You wouldn't find a fucking thing
For years I've been empty
And I've been numb to everything
So please stop with the advice

CLYDE HURLSTON

Pretending like everything's nice
When you were never there for me
So let me return to my hell!
But if you wish... you can...
Dig into my heart
And tell me what I've got left
'Cause living is this way
Isn't good for my health
Why can't I be happy
As I wallow in the mundane
Why am I left bitter
And defined by my shame...

A STRANGER'S ALLURE

In a dark-lit world,
Pierced with neon lights
So many search for love,
On these early morning nights
Cigarette smoke has replaced,
Fresh air on autumn days
And alcohol fuels the mind,
Leaving a cloud of drunken haze
And their love for the unknown,
Helps them forget what they have at home
They come crawling back to this,
To find something for their own
Pleasure, amusement,
Or maybe every sort
Balancing what they give and take,
It's the newest form of sport
They love the thrilling rush
Of the leaving things to chance
The lock eyes with an attractive stranger,
And thus begins the dance
Words aren't often spoken,
But sparks begins to fly
They feel something for this person,
And can't help but wonder why
While parting a sea of people,
They ride unseen waves of desire
Curiosity is a burning fire,
And the inferno slowly reaches higher
Everything they know,
Has become boring and mundane
And since the spark was lit,
They're like moths nearing an open flame
Their wings touching gently,
They engage in talk best described as sweet
Like when they left their nest,
They didn't intend to meet
A person like they've met tonight,

And other things pleasing to the ears
One orders another round of drinks,
To drown out any unwelcome fears
And down inside the glass,
They ignore the reflections of lovers past
Hoping that this momentary lapse
Of hindsight will forever last
And these two are not foolish in the least,
They're just two optimists
Crawling their way out of the grips of an imaginary beast
That many have labeled as a pessimist,
But that's my point of view,
And it's one that these two have surely missed
For their presents aren't weighed down,
By the shortcomings of yesterday
Even with the possibility of hearing "no" tomorrow,
They still say "yes" today
And I would lay down the burden of mine,
And promise to never hate bliss
If I could look into the eyes of the one,
Who made me feel like I was weightless
But alas, it seems I'll never enjoy the feeling,
Of an act so very pure
Maybe I should follow the lead
Of those who finally cave in to a stranger's allure.

ILLUMINATE

My mind's more different
Than it was yesterday
Requests met with no
But I said yes today
Submit my trust
To your ever-molding hands
As the hourglass
Fails to catch the sands
Am I the crow
To the left of the murder
Because I'd kill myself
Before I chose to hurt her
Maybe I'm diseased
For feeling like this
But to picture her smile
Means God truly does exist
So please smile at me
And illuminate the darkness
'Cause there is so much to see
And your point of view's the sharpest
Things gradually blur into one
When kept inside my eyes
And when the day's said and done
Will you still be my prize
You make me feel alive
When others left me numb
I'd lie awake at night
Wondering what I've become
A monster trapped inside
This prison made of fear
I don't care how long you stay
I'm just glad to have you here
Am I the crow
To the left of the murder
Because I'd kill myself
Before I chose to hurt her
Maybe I'm diseased

For feeling like this
But to picture her smile
Means God truly does exist
So please smile at me
And illuminate the darkness
'Cause there is so much to see
And your point of view's the sharpest
Things gradually blur into one
When kept inside my eyes
And when the day's said and done
Will you still be my prize
Am I the crow
To the left of the murder
Because I'd kill myself
Before I chose to hurt her
Maybe I'm diseased
For feeling like this
But to picture her smile
Means God truly does exist
So please smile at me
And illuminate the darkness
'Cause there is so much to see
And your point of view's the sharpest
Things gradually blur into one
When kept inside my eyes
And when the day's said and done
Will you still be my prize...

MEANINGLESS

The years are blurring into weeks
And no one seems to be aware
I can tell by the way he speaks
That he surely doesn't care
After all, he's on top the game
With hands full of hundred bills
He sells the product without shame
And he doesn't care who it kills
As the weeks blur into days
It seems that we have lost our ways
And no one else is seeing this
We're wasting time on what is meaningless
The days are blurring into blinks
And no one seems to be aware
And I can tell by the way she thinks
That she surely doesn't care
After all, she's thrown caution to the wind
Thinking he'll go the extra mile
Claims he forgot his glove again
And soon this girl shall bear his child
As the weeks blur into days
It seems that we have lost our ways
And no one else is seeing this
We're wasting time on what is meaningless
As the days blur into one
Why'd God give up His only son
To bleed out for us in vain
Does He regret each ounce of pain
If you were still up on that cross
Would you get down and guide the lost?
Or would you cry and hang your head in shame
When most of us just abuse your name
Are we too weak too live like you
And be crucified and still fight through
Tell me my Lord if you're seeing this
Have we made your sacrifice feel meaningless?
Because as the weeks blur into days
It seems that we have lost our ways
And no one else is seeing this
We're wasting time on what is meaningless...

REJOICE

With memories like movies
I watch them unfold
But they only move me
When the good parts are told
Because I drown out the bad
In a sea named naive
And it's the most fun I've had
That's what I do believe
Does it make me wrong
To block out these things
When I've spent too long
Feeling the pain that it brings
So forgive me my dear
If the glass is half-full
Rejoice! The wolves aren't here
They've thrown down their wool
The distance between us
Is ever-growing
And the Gods haven't seen us
Because you're never showing
What you hold inside
To anyone of them
And as people chip at your pride
Your outlook is grim
Does it make me wrong
To block out these things
When I've spent too long
Feeling the pain that it brings
So forgive me my dear
If the glass is half-full
Rejoice! The wolves aren't here
They've thrown down their wool
There are so many things to see
When you stop and look around
From every leaf on that tree
To the dirt that's on the ground
So many people rush to die

BROKEN SKY

That they don't slow down to live
And they don't understand why
It feels better to give...
If I could grow wings to fly
Would my past still hold me down?
If I would throw things and cry
Would I be in pieces on the ground?
Does it make me wrong
To block out these things
When I've spent too long
Feeling the pain that it brings
So forgive me my dear
If the glass is half-full
Rejoice! The wolves aren't here
They've thrown down their wool
Rejoice, the wolves are gone...
Rejoice, the wolves are gone...
Rejoice, the wolves are gone...
Oh my dear, it's been too long.

CLYDE HURLSTON

MY UNCROWNED QUEEN

Across this cold and storied land
Sits a humble abode
And with a map in my hand
I make my way down the road
With so many twists and turns
Before I'm due to arrive
At the home where the passion burns
Within the one who makes me feel alive...
There's a heart on my sleeve
That I proudly will wear
Because my dear I do believe
You're here to end my despair
So I will take these written notes
And for you I will sing them
While you're free to rule my heart
Since you don't have a kingdom
Just in the door she stands
In her finest satin dress
Hiding her face in her hands
Proclaiming her life is a mess
I place my hand beneath her chin
And raised her face to mine
As I said things will be fine again
We just have to give it time
There's a heart on my sleeve
That I proudly will wear
Because my dear I do believe
You're here to end my despair
So I will take these written notes
And for you I will sing them
While you're free to rule my heart
Since you don't have a kingdom
She asked me how I could be so sure
That things would go her way
And I said with intentions pure
That I am here today
To give you a crown

BROKEN SKY

That you can call your own
And deep within my heart
You can take your place,
Right on top your throne…
Yes, there's a heart on my sleeve
That I proudly will wear
Because my dear I do believe
You're here to end my despair
So I will take these written notes
And for you I will sing them
While you're free to rule my heart
Since you don't have a kingdom…

CLYDE HURLSTON

DREAMGIRL OVERDOSE

As her dress kissed the floor
She couldn't feel her burdens anymore
She just cried and danced
As if the song somehow romanced
Then she looked at me
As angelic as she could be
I wish I knew what she thought
But alas it seems it was for naught
'Cause she couldn't love me
While she's floating above me
She can't hear from way up there
And until she comes down
I'm holding my ground
She's gotta show me that she cares
As her dress kissed the wind
I knew she'd never let me in
To her mind, so unkind
I'm a puppet dancing on her line
She says move, so I do
And I scream 'til my face is blue
She offers a smile, and a wink
But doesn't care what I say or think
'Cause she couldn't love me
While she's floating above me
She can't hear from way up there
And until she comes down
I'm holding my ground
She's gotta show me that she cares
With her words flowing through my veins
And her kiss curing all my pains
I slowly go insane...
Out of body and mind,
Because she is truly divine,
And I'm running out of time...
'Cause she couldn't love me
While she's floating above me
She can't hear from way up there

BROKEN SKY

And until she comes down
I'm holding my ground
She's gotta show me that she cares
No, she couldn't love me
While she's floating above me
She can't fly and hold me close
But until she comes down
I'm holding my ground
A victim of a dreamgirl overdose...

BROKEN SKY

As these dark gray clouds
Shatter into pieces
The sea is like a blanket
With a thousand creases
I sit on top a perch so high
Beyond the reach of spoken lies
I love to fly through this broken sky
But I, I don't know why
I try my best,
To spread my wings
Try to make them touch,
Every single thing
As I fall down to the ground
I hit without a sound
And that's a sight you love to see
'Cause you've torn my wings,
Torn my wings from me...
I try to take flight again
To experience my freedom
And there are some people lost
From here I can see them
And then it starts to rain broken glass
The question why is what you ask
They're just pieces of my haunted past
Lain to rest at last
I try my best,
To spread my wings
Try to make them touch,
Every single thing
As I fall down to the ground
I hit without a sound
And that's a sight you love to see
'Cause you've torn my wings,
Torn my wings from me...
I sit on top a perch so high
Beyond the reach of your spoken lies
I love to fly through this broken sky...

BROKEN SKY

I try to take flight again
To experience my freedom
And there are some people lost
From here I can see them…
I try my best,
To spread my wings
Try to make them touch,
Every single thing
As I fall down to the ground
I hit without a sound
And that's a sight you love to see
'Cause you've torn my wings,
Torn my wings from me…

TAKE THIS HEART

If hope were a currency
I've defaulted on my loans
And so the same old void remains
I can feel it in my bones
And yet they tell me not to fret
'Cause help is on the way
But after thirty something years
This is all I have to say
You can save your sweet advice
And your tales of yesteryear
Because it's only loneliness
That seems to fester here
And friend, if you don't believe
You'd need only check my sleeve
Oh, will someone take this heart?
Since all it does it bleed
Your every status is a whip
Your every picture is a gun
And your silence is a knife
That I just can't outrun
And it seems you torture me
Right inside my memories
So since I cannot get away
I guess this is all I have to say
You can save your sweet advice
And your tales of yesteryear
Because it's only loneliness
That seems to fester here
And friend, if you don't believe
You'd need only check my sleeve
Oh, will someone take this heart?
Since all it does it bleed
Now I hate to sound like this
'Cause life ain't all that bad
But how are you supposed to feel
When misfortune's all you ever had
Is there a lesson trapped in this?

BROKEN SKY

What is life supposed to teach?
By placing everything I want
Just beyond my reach
You can save your sweet advice
And your tales of yesteryear
Because it's only loneliness
That seems to fester here
And friend, if you don't believe
You'd need only check my sleeve
Oh, will someone take this heart?
Since all it does it bleed
Friend, you can save your sweet advice
And the tales of yesteryear
'Cause now it's only misery
That seems to fester here
And if you still cannot believe
You can overlook my sleeve
And find a beat within this heart
That no longer wants to bleed...

CLYDE HURLSTON

AND SO WE REACH THE END AGAIN...

"There is something infinitely healing in the repeated refrains of nature - the assurance that dawn comes after night, and spring after winter."

-Rachel Carson

"Live in each season as it passes; breathe the air, drink the drink, taste the fruit, and resign yourself to the influence of the Earth."

-Henry David Thoreau

CLYDE HURLSTON

"A RAVEN IS BORN"
ART BY VALISA BERNARDINO

www.ingramcontent.com/pod-product-compliance
Lightning Source LLC
Chambersburg PA
CBHW072151100526
44589CB00015B/2176